Teachers must be taught to look for sensibility and feeling in their pupils, as well as the abilities to perform intellectual tasks. Teachers usually try too hard to interpet their pupil's work. If a child writes about violence he is looked upon as expressing violent impulses that are "really" within him. If he writes about loneliness his teacher tries to provide him with companionship. This usual view condescendingly implies that the child is incapable of literary exploration. Worse, it implies he is as humorless as the adults who assume responsibility for his education. I have laughed, cried, been duped, outraged, and sometimes bored by what my pupils have written—and I have told them this. Their effort to understand themselves and the things around them demands no less.

HERBERT R. KOHL
Teaching the "Unteachable"

Let Them Be Themselves

Language Arts Enrichment For Disadvantaged Children In Elementary Schools

Lee Bennett Hopkins, Formerly Senior Consultant, Educational Resources Center, Bank Street College of Education, New York City

Citation Press, New York • 1969

For reprint permission, grateful acknowledgement is made to:

Atheneum Publishers for "Balloons" by Patricia Hubbell. Copyright © 1968 by Patricia Hubbell from CATCH ME A WIND.

Doubleday & Company, Inc. for "What Is Brown?" by Mary O'Neill. From HAILSTONES AND HALIBUT BONES, by Mary O'Neill. Copyright © 1961 by Mary LeDuc O'Neill.

United States Department of the Interior for "The Navajo" by Ruby Frank and Phillip Kee. From SMOKE SIGNALS, February 1968.

Photo Credits:

Cover—Hella Hannid from Rapho Guillumette.

Inside—Marel Harayda; Morton R. Engelberg from The Ford Foundation; George Zimbel from Monkmeyer; John Shearer, 18, 1966 Scholastic Magazines—Kodak Photo Awards; Max Tharpe Photo Library; Arnold Talbott, 18, 1967 Scholastic Magazines—Kodak Photo Awards; Max Tharpe Photo Library.

Designed by June Martin

LIBRARY OF CONGRESS CATALOG CARD NUMBER 69-18130

Printed in the U.S.A.

To—and for—Misha

Who

Encouraged This and Saw It Through To The Very End

Foreword

TEACHERS HAVE LONG needed a book such as this. Though it is directed especially to the inner-city school language arts teacher, there is little here that would not be appropriate for use in classrooms anywhere. The great strength of this book is that it is filled with excellent suggestions for making the teaching-learning act more exciting, more significant, and more rewarding. These suggestions, though they are all supported by sound educational theory, do not come from some methods professor's theorizings; instead they come from classroom teachers who have tailored and tested them in inner-city and rural school situations and found them to be effective.

Certainly Mr. Hopkins, who is himself a well-known authority on inner-city schools, does not suggest that these classroom practices be implemented just as they are herein described. He knows, as does every good teacher, that the only classroom practices that really do the job are those the teacher has refined to suit his own teaching style and the learning styles of his particular students. It is equally obvious that the content of this volume is not offered as a substitute for a curriculum, though much of what is described is applicable to curriculum design; rather, these recommendations are intended to help the classroom teacher put into effect practices that will enrich the language arts curriculum for all children, and especially those who are disadvantaged.

In sum, the reader is offered scores of exciting ideas—to choose and pick among, to elaborate upon, and to innovate from—that will help him to build a more vigorous learning environment in his classroom.

SHELTON L. ROOT, JR.
Professor of English Education
College of Education
University of Georgia
Athens, Georgia

Contents

Words From A Fellow Educator

TEACHERS ARE PART of the momentous revolution that is taking place in America. In all sections of our country old institutional forms are being challenged; college campuses, suburbs, and cities all contribute to the cacophony of voices demanding change. Change is on every educator's lips—new mathematics, new social studies, new reading techniques. *Change!* Try the *new* basal readers, try the *new* kits, try i.t.a., try the phonics approach. Try! Experiment! Change!

The teacher as an educator can no longer be content with the methods of yesterday; he cannot remain static. Education is not what it was 15 or 30 years ago—or even what it was yesterday. Whether the teacher, parent, or citizen likes it or not, whether he is motivated or not, he must become part of the "in" society. He has to know about such happenings as the space race, the latest comic book or television hero, the mod-mode, the location of formerly obscure, underdeveloped nations half-way across the globe, and the demands of millions of our forgotten minorities who cry out for the resolution of old injustices.

Even children are rebelling today. Their hair is longer, their skirts are shorter, their music is louder, their protests are greater than they have ever been before, and the generation gap threatens to become an ever-widening chasm. Some adults say: "Kids today have everything! They have cars, color television sets, clothes, money." While it is true that some children have all this, many do not, and they eagerly demand to share in the affluence of America.

Young people today, both the disadvantaged, and the advantaged, are beset by a host of problems inherited from yesterday's young people who have aged and become parents, leaders, and educators: problems of the inner cities, integration, demands for technical skill as a condition for future employment, and enticements from every angle which say: "Come real close, but don't touch! Look, look, look! See, see, see! No! No! No!"

Clearly teachers today face an enormously difficult job. Society relies upon them to train tomorrow's wage earners, citizens, and parents. Teachers in twentieth century America have a difficult assignment but they do their job and hope for the best. *Let Them Be Themselves* was prepared with today's classroom teacher in mind. The book is a compilation of innovative activities and ideas that have been successfully tried and tested throughout the United States and Puerto Rico. It is a has-been-done book rather than a how-to-do book. Although this work is oriented toward the disadvantaged child, its contents apply to *all* children. By emphasizing language arts, which encompass the basic interests common to all mankind and aid him in communicating by speaking, listening, reading, and writing, the spectrum between the advantaged and the disadvantaged becomes a means through which all children can be themselves.

I sincerely hope that this text will help teachers-to-be, assist young teachers, and give experienced teachers some new ideas while working under the everyday pressures in our schools.

LEE BENNETT HOPKINS
New York, New York
September 1968

The Improvement of Self-Image
Who Are They?-Who Am I?

MANY LABELS ARE attached to disadvantaged children—socially disadvantaged, culturally disadvantaged, culturally deprived, underprivileged, educationally deprived, lower class, lower socio-economic strata, ghettoized children, the segregated, intellectually deprived, the bilingual child, the dialectal child, the migrant, the reservation child—and many reasons are cited as to *why* these children are disadvantaged and *how* they become that way. Many preventive and remedial programs are being carried out; some are effective and some are not.

Who are the disadvantaged in today's schools?

Where do they come from?

They are the Negro and the Puerto Rican children in the slum schools of the inner cities—Harlem in New York, Watts in Los Angeles, the Hough area of Cleveland, Bedford-Stuyvesant in Brooklyn. They also include children in poverty areas in all our major cities—Detroit, New Haven, Hartford, Chicago, Newark, Washington, Baltimore, San Juan, and Dade County. They are the children of the migrant workers who follow crops from place to place as a means of livelihood, traveling from the San Bernadino Valley in California to Long Island in New York. They are the children in the Appalachians and the Cumberlands, scattered throughout Kentucky, Virginia, and Tennessee, and they are the Indian children of Papagos, Arizona. They are the children who enter the United States from the West Indies, Cuba, Puerto Rico, Haiti, the Dominican Republic, and from South America—Chile, Ecuador, Argentina, Colombia, and Venezuela. They are the children who enter school with many strikes against them including:

- unstable family and home lives
- language barriers
- a very distorted view of the image of self.

Every child develops a picture of himself based on his interaction with family, peers, and environment. In the case of the disadvanged child, this picture is often distorted by the absence of a mother or father figure and society's apparent rejection of him through the device of discrimination. In addition, the limited job opportunities available to minority group adults sharply limits the adult roles the child is able to see and emulate.

Family environment and language handicaps can take years and years of patience and struggle to deal with, but improving the self-image of disadvantaged children cannot wait. Deliberate efforts must begin immediately to raise their sights. The Educational Policies Commission in its recent report, *Education and the Disadvantaged American* (Washington, D.C.: National Education Association, 1962, pp. 15-16), indicated that to be successful a school program must attack the problem of the disadvantaged on three fronts simultaneously:

1. It must demonstrate to pupils a close relationship between school and life.
2. It must include remedial services that will ensure academic progress.
3. It must arouse aspirations that can alter constructively the courses of young lives.

The following comments by children were recorded throughout the country in various schools with a one hundred percent population of disadvantaged children. These remarks illustrate some of the negative ideas and misconceptions these children have in regard to their place in society and to their heritage.

> SIXTH GRADE CHILD: Were there ever any colored cavemen?
> TEACHER: I am sure that there were. Why do you ask?
> CHILD: 'Cause there ain't never any pictures of colored cavemen in books. Only white cavemen. I don't think there ever was no colored cavemen!

> Two visitors from Oklahoma visited a fifth-grade classroom. One of the men was white, the other Negro. When they were introduced to the children, a girl called out to the Negro visitor: "You all can't be black! There ain't no black people in Oklahoma!"
> The gentleman assured her that there were black people in the state; however, the child could not accept his remarks. After a moment or two of deep thought, she stated: "You had to be born in Harlem first, and then go out to Oklahoma. Black people are born in Harlem before they go away from it!"

A fourth-grade child talking to his teacher asked: "Were you born white?"

The teacher replied, "Yes!"

"I was born white, too," stated the child, "but I turned Puerto Rican when I was one year old 'cause I was so bad!"

A third-grade migrant child stated: "People don't like us. That's why we have to move around a lot. People don't like pickers like me and my sister."

A second-grade child commented: "The difference between colored and white is the way you all act. We're colored because we're a bad lot, huh?"

An Indian child in the first-grade asks: "Teacher, who am I?"

The above are just a small sampling of the types of comments and responses children utter by the thousands day after day in classrooms near and far. Obviously, the child who feels that he or she is "a bad lot," that black means "bad," or that Spanish-speaking indicates ignorance, can only envision a limited future for himself. The classroom teacher, through the devices of trips, audio-visual aids, children's literature, and human resources can provide a broader horizon for the child who is locked in to the narrow boundaries of his immediate neighborhood. Acquainting children with past and contemporary figures of importance who are of their own particular race or national background can go a long way toward providing a child with a positive self-image.

To undo much of the damage that has been done is a complex task. We teachers must try, however, for we cannot afford to allow children to grow up into adulthood with such negative feelings, anxieties, and falsities about themselves and their roles in today's civilization. And we must not assume that building a positive self-concept is a concern only of the disadvantaged child. In today's mechanized world, a world filled with change, all children need the strength that a healthy self-concept can provide.

What can we teachers do?

How can we do it?

There are no pat answers. Experimentation, imagination, and determined effort can provide the means to help disadvantaged youth find their place in life. The techniques offered below have been used, and they have proved to be effective with disadvantaged children; they have been used as aids in improving self-image and to develop positive concepts of children's cultural and racial backgrounds.

Look in the Mirror

Many times disadvantaged children come from homes where the only mirror is in the bathroom. This mirror is usually on the medicine chest and far out of reach of the average child. Small wall mirrors or inexpensive full-length mirrors placed in classrooms and in corridors at a child's eye level give children the opportunity to really see themselves during the day—a privilege not afforded to many.

A variety of oral and written language activities have been sparked by the use of a mirror in the classroom. One second-grade teacher in an Appalachian classroom in Kentucky uses a mirror to have children role-play various parts. A large box is filled with hats of all kinds—a policeman's hat, a fireman's helmet, a nurse's cap, a sailor's cap, an astronaut's helmet, an airplane captain's hat, and an Indian headdress, along with many discarded hats that were worn by mommies and daddies—that have been collected through the years. The children don the hats and go to the mirror. With either the teacher or another student, a child takes on the role that the hat suggests, freely converses about duties and responsibilities, or just has a good time.

In another classroom where this concept was tried, the teacher had the children talk into a tape recorder, later writing out some of the comments. This served as the basis for an innovative bulletin board called "In Your Everyday Bonnet." The actual hats were fastened to a bulletin board with comments prepared by the children underneath each one. Several of the responses included:

Under the Nurse's Cap:
I must go now and take all the babies thermometers out of their mouths.

Under the Indian Headdress:
My chiefs are the best ones in the land. They bring me a heap of skins any time I want them.

Under a Flowery Bonnet:
This is my Easter bonnet. It took three years to make and it cost one million dollars, and that's a lot for a hat!

Besides having a chance to speak and listen, the boys and girls had the opportunity to see themselves in creative and imaginative roles.

A fourth-grade teacher in Hartford, Connecticut, uses the mirror to correlate science learnings with language

arts skills. He uses an excellent book, *Look At Your Eyes,**
to motivate such learnings. Children look into mirrors
and begin to really discover their own eyes. They look
at the color, the size, the shape, their eyebrows, eye-
lashes, and eyelids. They begin to discuss, to analyze,
and to think critically about something they had taken
for granted. The children talk, they write, they draw,
and they perform simple experiments to learn more about
themselves—to discover how different each person is,
yet how human beings are all so much the same.

Lights, Camera, Action

Photographs can be used in a variety of ways. Whenever possible, photographs should be taken of both individuals and groups in the classroom. One project going on in several schools in the Harlem area is based on
the imaginative use of the camera. Teachers use inexpensive box cameras and Polaroid cameras, where available, to catch children in the act of solving different
problems or of making a contribution to the class.
Pictures have been taken of children reading a book,
working on an art project, or performing work on the
chalkboard. Group shots were taken of teams "who
won the relay race" or of the group "who came in first

---

* Written by Paul Showers and illustrated by Paul Galdone in 1962,
this is part of "Let's-Read-and-Find-Out-Science" series published by
Thomas Y. Crowell, New York. The series is an excellent one that provides children with basic scientific information presented in a way
which young children can cope with. Many of the books have integrated
illustrations. Other books in the series include: *Your Skin and Mine,
Straight Hair, Curly Hair, How Many Teeth, My Five Senses,* and
My Hand.

in the spelling bee competitions." The camera also plays an important role during field trip excursions. Mounting the pictures in books and occasionally displaying them provided these children with an image of how they looked and acted in different candid situations.

The New York Times (April 25, 1968) recently reported on a photography project at Public School 36 in the Williamsburg section of Brooklyn, which is part of a program involving nine public schools and four community centers in slum areas throughout the city. The project, sponsored by the Horace Mann Institute of School Experimentation, at Teacher's College, Columbia University, and supported by an Eastman Kodak grant, was designed to give children who had difficulty in written communication another means of expression.

Children were supplied automatic cameras and film and were taken into the community to shoot whatever they pleased. Each child had the opportunity to take six shots. The children's teacher, Ray Vogel, built an entire curriculum around photography. He remarks: "A lot of things are said about these kids. They say they can't write, but they want to write about the pictures they take. These are children who had never done anything at all—zero! Now they've done something. They have taken pictures, some of them very good. It's given them at least one success under their belts, and after a life of so much failure that can mean everything."

The Sharing Box

A cardboard box became "the sharing box" in a non-English speaking second-grade. Books, toys, games, and hobbies, were put into the box for others to share during their free time. The contributor (or teacher) labeled each item by attaching a card with his name on it. Things shared were the basis for an oral language activity. Before items were placed in the box, children described them and/or told why they brought them in to share. The classroom teacher used the children's comments as a basis for writing experience charts. Each day she listed the children's contributions:

> Mario put a *top* in the box today.
> Dolores put a *book* in the box today.
> Juan put a *yo-yo* in the box today.

The children were able to learn many new words as a result of this activity; it also underlined the fact that every child has *something* worth giving.

The Welcome Back System

Children from disadvantaged areas are frequently absent from school. A welcome back system has been used in many schools very successfully. Each child in the class chooses a buddy. When one or the other is absent from school for a day or for a period of time, the buddy goes to visit the absentee to find out why he was out or to bring him home study assignments, or notices. If a child is out due to illness, the buddy reports to the teacher, and the class sends him a get-well card or letter. When the absent child returns to school, his buddy helps him to fit back into the regular daily routines of the classroom.

Creative Calendars

Children can do research to find famous birthdays, anniversaries, dates of inventions, and special holidays or events pertaining to a city, state, country, or race. With this information, weekly or monthly calendars can be created. "Puerto Rico: A Holiday Calendar" was prepared and mimeographed by consultants Annette Frank Shapiro and Marcella Williams, on the Bank Street College of Education staff, New York City, for use in East Harlem schools where a high percentage of the population is Spanish-speaking. Among the items included were:

JANUARY 11: This is a school holiday because it is the birthday of Eugenio Maria de Hostos. Hostos was a famous poet, educator, and political leader. In the schools, the children study his biography and learn about him as a writer and a politician. Flowers are placed at his monument at the University, and speeches are made in his honor.

APRIL 16: This school holiday is Jose de Diego Day. Diego was a famous poet and writer. Children learn about his life in school. Flowers are placed at his statue, and his poems are recited in the schools.

JUNE 24: San Juan Batista Day is an important day in San Juan because San Juan Batista is the patron saint of San Juan. Each town has its own patron saint. Some towns begin to celebrate the day dedicated to the saint as early as nine days before.

Special activities take place during this time. For example, one day may be devoted to games, songs, and dances or musical groups in the town plaza; another day may be devoted to boat races. Entertainers move from town to town during the year to help celebrate the 77 patron saints of each town.

This calendar was prepared with the sound philosophy that:

> Most children have grown up admiring heroes and heroines of their own country. Holidays based on their history and culture hold a special significance for them. When these heroes and heroines are discussed in the classroom as fine examples of leaders, then the children naturally feel more secure in a new situation. When their holidays are made part of the school year, the children achieve more status in the eyes of their peers. As a result, all the children in the class learn to respect and appreciate the contributions of other ethnic, racial, and social groups.

The calendar served to stimulate children in other schools and in other areas to create various types of calendars. Among these were "A Negro History Calendar," "South American Holidays," "People of the Islands," and "Great Inventions by Negroes."

Autobiographies

A one-page autobiography written by each child can be put into a scrapbook and bound, or they can be placed around the room. This technique has been beneficial in introducing the children to student teachers, substitute teachers, teacher aides, and the many visitors who come in and out of an elementary classroom during the school year. Children also get to know about one another, and they enjoy reading about themselves. A picture of each child to accompany his autobiography is a worthwhile addition.

Who Is the Child of the Week?

Each week of the school year a child in every class-room can be selected as The Child of the Week. Names can be drawn from a box, or it can be decided that children will be selected alphabetically by last name. The child selected prepares a bulletin board display to tell the class about himself. We can draw from many sources—writing exercises, drawings, or photographs can tell about his specific interest in sports, television shows, hobbies, pets, or books. The child's address and a list of his family members might also be posted. When possible, a member of The Child of the Week's family—either a parent or a younger or older brother or sister who attend the same school—should be invited to the class to see his display. This idea has been used and implemented as a motivating device for interest in class-room and school affairs. It also serves to build up the self-image of even the slowest child in the classroom.

Hall of Fame

A Hall of Fame has been used in two ways. First, several schools have utilized this project to raise the children's occupational sights by having former graduates elected to their school's Hall of Fame. People chosen are those who have distinguished themselves in various fields and represent sports and entertainment personalities or business and industry leaders as well as people in various professions. One school Hall of Fame boasts of a fashion designer for a leading department store, a scenic designer for the theater, an author, and a popular singing group. Each time a new member is added, a special ceremony that involves both the school and the community is planned.

Secondly, classroom Halls of Fame have been developed. The children research famous personalities for candidacy into the Hall of Fame. Campaigning can be done by individuals or by groups of children. The class can vote by secret ballot whether or not new members are to be honored. This type of activity can be an interesting one for children to carry out, for *they* can decide on rules and regulations for the operation of the project. Among classroom Halls of Fame selected by children have been A Contemporary Negro Hall of Fame, which included Dr. Martin Luther King, Jr., Ralph David Abernathy, Carl B. Stokes, Leslie Uggams, and The Supremes; A Sports Hall of Fame which featured baseball heroes Babe Ruth and Willie Mays, basketball champion Wilt Chamberlain, and tennis star Althea Gibson; and A Music Hall Fame, which included Leonard Bernstein, Pablo Casals, and the Beatles.

So It's Their Birthday!

The most important days of any school year are the children's birthdays. No matter what age the child is, he wants his day to be remembered and shared with others. The following activities can be adapted for the various grades and can give a new look to the old custom of birthday celebrations.

Birthday Charts

In a Washington, D.C., classroom, early in the school year, each child tape records his name and birthdate.

This information is transcribed and placed on oak tag charts showing the days from September to August. When a special day arrives, activities are planned to make that child feel proud of *his day*. Some children select a favorite poem to read; others relate something of interest, perhaps about where they were born, early childhood memories, or a hobby. Other children become messengers for the day or choose the game they enjoy most for the period of physical education. Class members make original cards for the child whose birthday is being celebrated and present them to him at the close of the school day.

The oak tag charts can take on a variety of themes and can be placed around the room for permanent display. Twelve trains cut from colored oak tag and labeled for each month can be connected on, above, or under a bulletin board to form Our Birthday Express. A small photograph of each child can be placed on the proper train. The same idea can be used to tie in with classroom interests. Rocket ships can lead to The Birthday Planet; stars can become A Sky of Birthdays; flowers can produce A Garden of Birthdays.

This Is Your Life

Committees might plan a booklet about each child's life. Discussions can be held as to what is involved in the creation of a biography. Each committee can then set out to explore and investigate highlights of the child's life. They might write letters to parents, interview friends and relatives, or gather information from former teachers. With the collected data, and perhaps interesting photographs, they can prepare an attractive booklet and present it to the birthday boy or girl.

The Birthday Box

Several art and/or writing sessions might be planned to allow children to produce gift articles for The Birthday Box. On a child's birthday he can select a gift from the box while the class sings "Happy Birthday." A discussion can be held about who wrote or made the gift and why. Through this activity young children of ten have the opportunity to feel proud—whether they are giving the gift or receiving it.

Birthday Books

If possible, it is desirable to have on hand one or several volumes of poems about birthdays to share with the class. Below is a selected list of some current and popular books for boys and girls:

Banner, Angela. *Happy Birthday with Ant and Bee*. New York: Watts, 1964.
Ant and Bee, two delightful characters, introduce the names of the days of the week, as they prepare for Kind Dog's birthday. The names of the various days are printed in red, which can encourage the children to participate while the teacher is reading the story.

Brewton, John E. and Sara, comp. *Birthday Candles Burning Bright: A Treasury of Birthday Poetry*. New York: Macmillan, 1960.
A fine collection of poems about birthdays, christenings, growing up, youth, and age. A special section is devoted to Christmas.

Hoban, Russell. *A Birthday for Frances*. New York: Harper & Row, 1968.

Frances' little sister Gloria is going to have a birthday. However, Frances is not too happy with all the fuss being made. This is a delightful picture book with lovely pictures by Lillian Hoban of Frances and the rest of her badger family.

Massie, Diane Redfield. *A Birthday for Bird*. New York: Parents' Magazine Press, 1966.

A bird's birthday is next week, and he hopes that all his friends will remember the day.

Rinkoff, Barbara M. *Birthday Parties Around the World*. New York: M. Barrows, 1967.

Recipes, games, favors, decorations, and birthday customs of 23 countries are described.

Scott, Ann Herbert. *Big Cowboy Western*. New York: Lothrop, Lee and Sheperd, 1965.

Martin, a young Negro boy, celebrates his fifth birthday by receiving "a cowboy hat and a holster with two silver guns." With this present, he sets out to do a real cowboy's job in the big city where he lives.

Seuss, Dr. *Happy Birthday to You!* New York: Random House, 1959.

The Great Birthday Bird of Katroo is on hand to help celebrate the Day of Days. Dr. Seuss' amusing verse and illustrations will delight any birthday child.

Wilson, John and Julia. *Becky*. New York: Thomas Y. Crowell, 1966.

Becky, a young Negro girl, wants to buy a doll which is $2.00 more than she received for her birthday.

Much research in the area of self-concept is still desperately needed for the sequence through which the self-image is developed is not completely known or understood. However, all the above devices are practical means of helping a child to see himself more clearly. They do not involve the expenditure of vast sums of money for fancy machines and/or equipment; they are techniques that build upon the natural endowments granted to all children—a name, a birthday, an image, a self! The educator working in cooperation with other teachers, a school system, a neighborhood, or parents can create endless possibilities for strengthening the growth potential of young children. Perhaps if they try, implement, and elaborate upon some of the ideas presented here, children will acquire more accurate views of themselves and will not pose such questions as that of the Indian youngster who asked plaintively: "Teacher, who am I?"

For Further Reading:

Burchinal, Lee G., ed. *Rural Youth in Crisis: Facts, Myths, and Social Change.* Washington, D. C.: United States Department of Health, Education and Welfare, 1965.

The material in this book is a condensed version of papers originally prepared as background for the Conference on Problems of Rural Youth in a Changing Environment, sponsored by the National Committee for Children and Youth. The papers presented are by leading experts in the field of educational psychology and sociology.

Conklin, Paul. "Proud of Being an Indian," *Scholastic Teacher,* March 28, 1968, pp. 10–11.

The article discusses ways in which Navaho children are given a sense of self-identity at the Rough Rock Denron School in Arizona.

Dentler, Robert A., Mackler, Bernard, and Warshauer, Mary Ellen, eds. *The Urban R's.* New York: Frederick A. Praeger, Inc., 1967.

Eighteen articles in this volume focus on the school and community and how they can provide a meaningful education for the city's children.

Frost, Joe L., and Hawks, Glenn R., eds. *The Disadvantaged Child: Issues and Innovations.* Boston: Houghton Mifflin, 1966.
An excellent, timely book of readings that give many practical suggestions for every level of the educational process. One chapter is devoted to "Teaching Communicative and Problem-Solving Skills."

Hopkins, Lee Bennett. "Back to School, Back to School! How Will We Know Just Who Is Who?" *The Instructor,* August/September 1967, pp. 108, 110.
Eight practical ideas are offered to "break the classroom ice and (to) aid both teachers and children in getting to know the new fold."

— Kohl, Herbert. *36 Children.* New York: New American Library, 1967.
The author writes a realistic account of a year of teaching Negro and Puerto Rican sixth-graders in a Harlem School.

Lewis, Claudia. *Children of the Cumberland.* New York: Columbia University Press, 1946.
The way of life of families living in the Cumberland Plateau in Tennessee is well-presented. Dramatic photographs of the people are included.

Lloyd, John. "Indian Education: Another National Problem," *Scholastic Teacher,* March 28, 1968, pp. 4–5.
The author interviews Charles N. Zellers, Assistant Commissioner of Education for the Bureau of Indian Affairs. The article provides some insights into the solutions of the problems of Indian education.

Miel, Alice with Kiester, Edwin, Jr. *The Short Changed Child of Suburbia.* New York: Institute of Human Relations Press, 1967.
An interesting paperback telling how to prepare suburban youth, who have inadequate opportunities for contact with in-

dividuals of other races, other generations, or other income levels, to live in our diverse society.

Passow, A. Henry, ed. *Education in Depressed Areas.* New York: Teachers College Press, Columbia University, 1963.
A book of readings emphasizing the psychological and sociological aspects of education in depressed areas.

Schrag, Peter. "Appalachia: Again the Forgotten Land." *Saturday Review,* January 27, 1968, pp. 14–18.
A new look at some of the old problems the people of Appalachia must still cope with.

Strom, Robert D., ed. *The Inner-City Classrooms Teacher Behaviors.* Columbus: Charles E. Merrill Books, 1966.
Ten leading specialists suggest specific ways to improve the teaching of disadvantaged children in urban areas.

Teaching About the Negro in United States History: A "Scholastic Teacher" Report. Englewood Cliffs, N.J.: Scholastic Magazines, Inc., 904 Sylvan Avenue, 1968, 16 pp. 25¢.
Articles, plus bibliographies of books, films, filmstrips, and records.

Trubowitz, Sidney. *A Handbook for Teaching in the Ghetto School.* Chicago: Quadrangle Books, Inc., 1968.
A practical and compassionate guide for teachers in ghetto schools written by a Harlem principal.

Children's Literature
A Journey To The Land Of Fiction

MOST CHILDREN AND ADULTS can recognize that the rhymes

> There was an old woman who lived in a shoe,
> She had so many children she didn't know what to
>   do . . .

and

> Peter, Peter, pumpkin eater,
> Had a wife and couldn't keep her . . .

are from the favorite mother in all literature—Mother Goose. Mother Goose, long an important figure in our literary heritage, has been dealt with in every conceivable way in books for children. Since 1697 when Charles Perrault published a collection of nursery tales entitled *Histoires Ou Contes du Temps Passé* and captioned a picture on the frontispiece "Contes de ma Mère l'Oye" (Tales of Mother Goose), the character has ap-

peared and reappeared in every major language. Countless English and American editions have been published
year after year and have been illustrated by the top
artists in the field of children's literature. Illustrators
such as Feodor Rojankovsky, Tasha Tudor, Roger Duvoisin, Marguerite de Angeli, Beni Montrèsor, and Ed
Emberly have given their time and talent to interpreting
the rhymes of old.

This is one of the wonderful qualities about books for
children—they rarely go out of date. Many of the books
written and published during the nineteenth and early
twentieth centuries are more popular now than they
were when they first appeared. Consider this list:

1843: *A Christmas Carol* by Charles Dickens
1846: *The Fairy Tales of Hans Christian Andersen*
1865: *Alice's Adventures in Wonderland* by Lewis
Carroll
1869: *Little Women* by Louisa May Alcott
1884: *Huckleberry Finn* by Mark Twain
1894: *The Jungle Book* by Rudyard Kipling
1908: *Wind in the Willows* by Kenneth Grahame

These are just a few of the many books that were
milestones in the field of literature for children, and it
is not surprising that these are books that have lasted.
Think of how many millions of children and adults have
come to know and love characters such as Tom Thumb,
Alice and her weird and fanciful friends, Huck and Tom,
and Mole and Ratty. Think of the million of youngsters
who have shared heartaches with the March family when
Beth dies at a young age, or those who have shared their
compassion with the Ugly Duckling.

Many recent books have much of the same quality

as the literary classics above. Characters such as Johnny in Lynd Ward's *The Biggest Bear,* Max in Maurice Sendak's *Where the Wild Things Are,* Peter in *The Snowy Day* by Ezra Jack Keats, Mario and his friends in George Selden's *The Cricket in Times Square,* Charlotte and her barnyard companions in E. B. White's *Charlotte's Web,* and Gilberto in Marie Hall Ets' *Gilberto and the Wind* will be around to delight and entertain children who were born mere hours ago.

The May 1967 *The New York Times Book Review, Children's Book Supplement* cited the ten best juvenile sellers in an analysis showing the sales ratings of the titles sold since the first of the year, based on reports from bookstores in 64 communities in the United States.

CHILDREN'S BEST SELLERS

1. *Charlotte's Web* by E. B. White. This wise, beautifully spun fable has been a perennial best seller since 1952.
2. *Up a Road Slowly* by Irene Hunt. Set in a small midwestern town, this sharply perceptive novel of a girl growing to maturity received the 1967 Newbery Award.
3. *Winnie-the-Pooh* by A. A. Milne. The story about Christopher Robin and his companions, first published in 1926, comes in many editions and adaptions.
4. *Sam, Bangs and Moonshine* by Evaline Ness. The illustrations for this picture book about a fisherman's daughter won the 1967 Caldecott Medal.
5. *A Friend Is Someone Who Likes You* by Joan Walsh Anglund. Friendship is where you find it is the theme of this 1958 book by the popular author-illustrator.

6. *Rabbit Hill* by Robert Lawson. Charming, whimsical, and prize-winning tale of animals in the Connecticut countryside (1944).

7. *Richard Scarry's Best Word Book Ever.* For the youngest, an illustrated dictionary of "things"—fruits, flowers, colors, clothes, shapes and sizes, etc. (1963).

8. *The Children's Bible.* A retelling, in a colorfully illustrated volume, of stories from the Old and New Testaments (1965).

9. *The Little Prince* by Antoine de Saint-Exupéry. Parable, allegory, fairy tale, many things, at once exquisite and elusive by the French author and flyer (1943).

10. *Wind in the Willows* by Kenneth Grahame. In several editions, the enduring English classic about Toad, Mole, and other animal friends (1908).

The list is oddly enough a potpourri of old and new —titles range from several years old to the 60-year-old *Wind in the Willows!*

Questions often asked by adults include: What do children *look for* in books? What *interests* them? What do I do when a child says: "Gimme a *good book* to read!" Is there any criteria for judging quality in children's books?

Children and adults seek the same qualities in books —they want a book that has a strong plot, plenty of action, and "happenings." They want to read a story they can identify with, one with realistic characters who seem true-to-life. Children want books that enable them to understand the different cultures and customs they encounter in life. This need can be met by many of today's books. Publishing trends definitely reflect the times in which we live. The Soviet Union's launching of Sputnik in 1957 was an integral influence in America's mass production of science books for children.

In the 1960's the impact of civil rights movements, the wave of Spanish-speaking peoples who came into the mainland, and the poverty programs and the resources and monies given by the federal government to combat growing social problems of minority groups and of impoverished areas provided the impetus for publishing material that reflected the disadvantaged child and the real world in which he lives. Prior to the 1960's, only a handful of books about minority cultures were evident. There is a great need for additional material of this type, for books play a vital role in the development of both understanding others and understanding self (see Appendix I: The Urban and Disadvantaged Child: A Booklist for Children.

Get and Give the Very Best

Certain styles of writing appeal to children; they often enjoy books written by the same author or books of the same type:

> There is a story about a little boy who had spent hours of satisfaction with *Blueberries for Sal,* by Robert McCloskey. One day he approached the librarian at the children's division and asked hopefully: "Do you have any more books about little kids picking things?" His delight in the story, his reassurance through its theme, and his enchantment with the pictures led the boy to call for more.[1]

---

1. Helen W. Painter. "Robert McCloskey: Master of Humorous Realism," *Elementary English,* February 1968, pp. 145-58.

It is not uncommon for children to read series after series of books or collections of books by one author. Many children know Dr. Seuss for his fanciful creations, Marguerite Henry for her exciting tales of horses, and Genevieve Foster for her biographies of famous people in history. They ask for books by certain authors knowing that they will find something similar to what they read before and something that will be just right for them.

The best criteria for selecting children's books is set by the child himself. He will quickly put down a book that does not appeal to him, is too hard for him to read, or is not right for the particular moment. There are many cases where teachers, librarians, and reviewers have praised a book highly, yet when used with children, it became deadwood! Boys and girls know what they like—and they only read voluntarily material that suits their moods and fancies.

This does not mean, however, that adults should not direct youngsters to books of quality. Children's literature is cluttered with mediocre volumes. We must guide children in their reading preferences and introduce them to the excellent books they might miss. Many lives can be made richer and fuller if we know children and know their books. If we do, we will have the right book, at the right time, for the child who states: "Teacher, gimme a good book!"

The twentieth century is indeed the era of children's literature, and there are more volumes being published now than ever before in history. With this explosion, however, teachers must know where to begin to look for material that will meet the needs of their children and how they can continue to gain information about new trends in books, new authors, and new materials. In a field that has become so rich, so quickly, it is necessary to have a basic knowledge of where to look. The sources discussed below have been selected to aid you on your quest to get and give the very best.

Award Winning Books

There are two major awards presented annually in the United States in the field of children's literature—the Newbery and the Caldecott awards (lists of the books receiving these awards appear in Appendix II: Caldecott and Newbery Award Winning Books). The Newbery Medal is presented to the author of "the most distinguished contribution to American literature for children." It is named for John Newbery, an eighteenth century publisher and bookseller. The Caldecott Medal, named after Randolph Caldecott, a famous English illustrator of books for children, is presented to the artist "of the most distinguished American picture book for children." These books should be in every school library collection, and children should be made aware of these annual award-winning volumes. The disadvantaged child particularly should not be deprived of these superbly written and illustrated books. Too often schools in disadvantaged areas do not secure these books but rather stock inferior, low reading-level texts.

Teachers should familiarize themselves with the titles and use them when ever an opportunity arises. A study of the United States will be greatly enriched with books such as *Caddie Woodlawn, The Matchlock Gun, Daniel Boone,* and *Johnny Tremain.* During the winter season many discussions can grow out of volumes such as *The Big Snow, White Snow, Bright Snow, The Snowy Day, Nine Days to Christmas,* and *Baboushka and the Three Kings.* To stretch young imaginations *The Voyages of Dr. Dolittle, The Twenty-One Balloons,* and *Where the Wild Things Are* should be read over and over again.

Children can be encouraged to create their own book awards. They can set criteria, make nominations, and then vote for the books they feel are best. Criteria can center around special themes or topics, fiction or non-fiction books, volumes of poetry, or books about special places or regions.

Periodicals

BOOKBIRD: This quarterly magazine, published by the International Institute for Children's, Juvenile, and Popular Literature, features: "Literature for Children and Young People," "News from all over the World," and "Recommendations for Translation." A subscription to the journal can be obtained from Package Library of Foreign Children's Books, 119 Fifth Avenue, New York, New York 10003, for $3.80 per year.

THE CALENDAR: This is a quarterly publication available from Children's Book Council, 175 Fifth Avenue, New York, New York 10010. A $1.00 fee will put you on the mailing list. Features include: "In and Around the Children's Book World," "Books and Dates," "Awards and Prizes," and "Materials and Publications Available."

ELEMENTARY ENGLISH: This journal dealing with language arts is published monthly, from October through May, by the National Council of Teachers of English, 508 South Sixth Street, Champaign, Illinois 61820; the subscription rate is $7.00 per year. Besides a monthly column, "Books for Children," edited by Shelton L. Root, Jr., it features articles on authors, illustrators, special books, and interests of children pertaining to books.

THE HORN BOOK: This journal is "about children's books and reading." It is published in February, April, June, August, October, and December and features articles on authors, illustrators, and recent books. The subscription rate is $6.00 per year and is available from The Horn Book, Inc., 585 Boylston Street, Boston, Massachusetts 02116.

SCHOLASTIC TEACHER: This publication appears weekly from September to June. A unique evaluation-reviewing service was initiated in 1965, in which panels of teachers, librarians, and curriculum specialists from grades pre-kindergarten through twelve try out books, as well as other media, in classrooms and then prepare reviews. These reviews are accummulated in an annual paperback entitled *New Educational Materials*, edited by Mary L. Allison and selling for $2.75. It is published by Citation Press, 904 Sylvan Avenue, Englewood Cliffs, New Jersey 07632; *Scholastic Teacher* may be ordered from the same address for $5.00 per year.

SCHOOL LIBRARY JOURNAL: Subtitled "The Magazine for Children's, Young Adult, and School Libraries," this journal is available from R. R. Bowker Company, 1180 Avenue of the Americas, New York, New York 10036. It appears monthly from September to May; subscription price is $5.00 annually. The journal features topical articles on children's literature as well as a section called "The Book Review," which reviews books for Pre-School and Primary Grades, Grades 3-6, Junior High Up, Brief Mention, and Books for Young Adults. The reviews are well annotated with stars and double stars given to those books above average and those recommended for first purchase.

TOP OF THE NEWS: Published in November, January, April, and June, this journal features articles on children's literature and reviews books, media, and professional material. The subscription rate is included in membership dues of the Children's Services Division and Young Adult Service Division of the American Library Association, 50 East Huron St., Chicago, Ill. 60611.

Newspapers

During Children's Book Week each November, most newspapers feature special sections on children's books. *The New York Times, The Denver Post, The Washington Post, The San Francisco Examiner & Chronicle, Boston Herald Traveler,* and *The Cleveland Press* are examples of excellent sources to look through for current reviews of recently published books. Children can be encouraged to write letters to these newspapers in late October asking that copies of the special supplements and reviews be sent to their classrooms prior to Children's Book Week. Youngsters can also look through local newspapers for special book sections. Interesting bulletin board displays can be made, built around pictures from book jackets and illustrations from the books and pictures of authors that children have clipped from the supplements. Files of this material can be kept for future use.

Other Sources

Individual publishing houses provide good sources of information about children's books, particularly new books. Twice a year catalogs are distributed giving titles, annotations, prices, and grade levels of new volumes. A good way for a teacher to become acquainted with new authors and trends in publishing is to ask to be placed on mailing lists and then browse through the catalogs received. Many publishing houses also distribute excellent material for classroom use such as posters, book jackets, bookmarks, and information about authors. *The Calendar* is one place where much of this free and/or inexpensive material is listed.

Bookstores, public libraries, and school libraries also provide material on books. Catalogs, special bibliographies, and book displays are usually available for teachers to use.

Reading to Children

Children love to be read to. They love to sit and listen to stories, anecdotes, and tales of long ago. They love to laugh together, cry together, imagine together, and go on wild, carefree adventures together. Any classroom teacher who has had the experience of sharing a chapter a day from an ongoing book knows how wonderful such an experience can be. Teachers of all children should read to their classes every day. Five or 10 minutes should be found and set aside for sharing the beautiful language that can be found in print. Books read aloud can speak many interests, can encourage children to read more by themselves, and can aid in developing a taste for fine literature.

Teachers of early grades seem to read more readily to children. In the nursery, in kindergarten classrooms, and in grades one through three, it seems as natural to read to children as it does to turn on the lights. Middle-grade youngster's however, are often neglected. Older boys and girls need this type of communication just as much as younger children do.

There are many excellent books to read to older children—many which they might miss if they are not read aloud. Complete stories, portions of books, even short descriptive passages might be read to spark further interests. Parts of *Johnny Tremain* or *Amos Fortune: Free Man* might be selected to whet appetites or just to acquaint children with selections of excellent prose.

Children in disadvantaged areas rarely know what it is like to be read to. Working parents cannot take the time to sit and read stories aloud, and many parents cannot read well themselves. These children, therefore, have very little opportunity to observe an adult family member engaged in reading activities. A teacher who regularly reads to his class several minutes a day can provide this important experience that is lacking in so many children's lives.

An excellent 24-minute, 16mm, sound-color film entitled *The Pleasure is Mutual* has been produced to show the many values derived from reading aloud.[2] Ten picture-book programs showing a variety of reading techniques in both urban and suburban areas are shown. Accompanying the film is "A Beginning Book List" and an excellent handbook, *How to Conduct Effective Picture Book Programs.* Although the film focuses on programs for three- to six-year-olds, the techniques illustrated can be adapted to any grade level. Experienced or new teachers will learn a great deal from viewing *The Pleasure Is Mutual.*

Read-Aloud Service Clubs

Read-Aloud Service Clubs have proved to be very successful with disadvantaged children. This project involves having older children read to younger children and was developed so that kindergarten, first-, second-, and third-graders might see their peers in a somewhat intellectual role rather than in monitorial roles, such as hall guard, office monitor, or eraser cleaner. Teachers as well as children found this service one that is exciting and beneficial. Lower- and upper-grade teachers held meetings to initiate the clubs. They agreed to set aside a specific hour each week for children to participate in this activity, they worked out ways to give critical appraisal to the readers, and they organized committees of teachers *and* students to select appropriate books to be used with the young children.

---

2. For further information on this film write to The Children's Books Council, 175 Fifth Avenue, New York, New York 10010.

The method was simple. A child in an upper grade was assigned to read or tell a story to a lower-grade class. Other children in his class accompanied the storyteller and implemented his demonstration with artwork, puppetry, creative dramatics, or audio-visual aids. An interesting sideline, not realized when this project was initiated, was that slow-learners in the fifth-and sixth-grade classrooms could peruse easy-to-read books and materials without losing face. These children can participate in a Read-Aloud Service Club and contribute to it in many ways.

Teachers of the upper-grades planned practice sessions in their classrooms, in which their students read to one another and discussed the salient points of good storytelling. Charts were then made to record such points as how to read a story effectively, how to pronounce words, how to use tone and pitch in one's voice, and ways in which the reader might animate the particular story he chose to read. These charts were then posted to serve as constant reminders as to what makes a good reader or teller of stories. The Read-Aloud Service Club was then ready to be launched within the school.

Many benefits evolved from this service—older children had the chance to renew acquaintances with favorite books, it provided an incentive for going to the library, it encouraged students to choose, review, and evaluate books for use with younger children, it created a need for good oral speaking habits, and it developed responsibility in everyone involved with its operation.

Hundreds of books were shared, more were reviewed, and children of all ages, grade levels, and achievement levels profited from this unique service.

Read-Aloud Film Aids

A recent innovation in language arts programs is "The Reading Incentive Film" series produced by the Communications Laboratory of Bank Street College of Education. These 16mm films are actually books-on-film and show personalities from the entertainment world reading directly into the camera. The camera alternates between shots of the reader and close-ups of the book he is reading. The original illustrations and strong action words and descriptive phrases are emphasized. The technicolor films include: Harry Belafonte reading both *Gilberto and the Wind* (a story by the Caldecott award-winner Marie Hall Ets, which tells of a Spanish-American boy and his friend, the wind) and *My Dog Is Lost* by Ezra Jack Keats and Pat Cherr (the story of Juanito, a newly arrived child from Puerto Rico and the problems of communication he has to face when Pepito gets lost in New York City); Shirley MacLaine reading *Noisy Nancy Norris* by Lou Ann Gaeddart (a delightful romp about a noisy Nancy living in an apartment house); and James Garner reading *What Kind of Feet Does a Bear Have?* (an exploration of similes, puns, metaphors, riddles, and paradoxes of a child's world).

These films have been used in many ways with different age groups. In addition to arousing children's interest in reading, the series has been field tested with teachers and teacher trainees to improve their oral reading skills, with parents to encourage them to read aloud to children, and with non-English speaking children who profited from hearing the sounds of the English language while seeing the words in print.

The films, 20 in all, are distributed through McGraw-Hill Text Films, 330 West 42nd Street, New York, New York 10036, and are available for purchase, rent, or to preview. A copy of the actual book is included with each film for further motivation.

A second innovation in filmmaking is the iconographic technique of motion picture photography perfected by Morton Schindel of the Weston Woods Studio. This procedure also retains the book's original illustrations but gives the illusion of motion. Sound effects, original musical scores, and excellent narrations are blended together to produce delightful results. Included in the long list of Weston Woods' pictures are these perennial favorites: *Caps for Sale* by Esphyr Slobodkina, *The Five Chinese Brothers* by Claire Bishop and Kurt Wiese, *Make Way for Ducklings* by Robert McCloskey, and *Millions of Cats* by Wanda Gag.

Schindel has also created films using live action. One of his most popular is a 27-minute color version of Robert McCloskey's *Homer Price*—a film that would appeal to any child in upper-elementary grades.

Other material produced at Weston Woods includes sound filmstrip sets, records, books, and special film programs. A complete catalog and information on the services can be obtained from Weston Woods, Weston, Connecticut 06880.

Filmstrip Sets and Recordings

Many companies produce excellent sound filmstrip

sets of books and stories for children. Boys and girls enjoy being able to look at and hear a story, either alone, in a small group, or with the entire class. Filmstrips and records provide an added advantage—they permit a child to look at a particular image as long as he wishes or to return to a particular part of the story over and over again. Children are also able to hear correct pronunciation and intonations of various words and phrases. This is particularly beneficial to the child for whom English is a second language.

Sound effects can stimulate children who may never have experienced things in life that adults sometimes take so much for granted. The roar of the hurricane winds in *Time of Wonder* or the diverse sounds of the sea in *Wheel on the School* may be strange sounds to many city children, yet to others may be familiar links to the island homes where the sea is a way of life.

Filmstrip and record equipment is more readily available than motion picture equipment. Small, inexpensive viewers can be placed on a desk or table, and earphones can be plugged into recording machines for individual viewing and listening. An additional advantage is the ability to reshow materials to children who have been absent or out of class.

Record-book combinations are innovative devices produced by Folkway/Scholastic Records, 906 Sylvan Avenue, Englewood Cliffs, New Jersey 07632. These sets contain long-playing records and paperback books. The philosophy behind their production is that children improve their reading skills when they combine listening with reading. *The Story of Ferdinand* is one title in this series. The following excerpt from the November/December 1967 *See Saw Books Memo to Teachers* summarizes the ingenuity that goes into the making of these sets:

> *The Story of Ferdinand* is a delightful tale about a Spanish bull who is selected for a Spanish national event—the bull fight. The story contains references to Spanish customs, sights and sounds, words and songs— and so we chose a gentleman with a Spanish accent to read it on a record. The story sounded better that way. It sounded more authentic, more colorful, and, we hope, more delightful.
>
> We added some songs in Spanish on the other side because they fitted the mood of the story. They are happy, simple, familiar, noisy songs, just right for all young children to hop to, dance to, play to, and respond to.
>
> But the final results are equal to much more than the sum of the parts. For Ferdinand is truly a very special record—a record that provides valuable opportunities for children to share many "precious differences" with each other. For the American child, here is a chance to learn something new about the language, customs, costumes, music, even the cuisine of the Spanish people. The Spanish-speaking child, in turn, shares his knowledge of another language with his peers. He has a much-needed opportunity to take pride in his cultural heritage, to identify with the narrator, to be an important part of something that brings pleasure and creative activity into his classroom.

Other companies that produce high quality film-strip-record sets include: Guidance Associates, Post Office Box 5, Pleasantville, New York 10570; Jam Handy Organization, 2821 East Grand Boulevard, Detroit, Michigan 48211; McGraw-Hill Text Films, 330 West 42nd Street, New York, New York 10036; and Society for Visual Education, 1345 Diversey Parkway, Chicago, Illinois 61614. The aforementioned distributors will glady place teachers' names on their mailing lists to receive current catalogs.

All children should be encouraged to read, but having an adult read to him on occasion—either live or through audio-visual media—is magic performed before his eyes. He does not have to struggle with the printed page, he does not have to wonder what certain words mean— he can just sit back, listen, and enjoy a pleasurable reading experience. One of the richest moments a teacher can have is for a child to come back years later and remark: "I'll never forget the time when we first heard of the book . . ." or "Remember the time when you read us the part where Beth died, and the whole class cried?"

Storytelling

Storytelling is a most effective way of enriching the lives of children in the elementary grades and of leading them to books. A teacher who has a wide variety of stories up his sleeve can, at a moment's notice, shake his cuff and speak words that will sprinkle fairy dust over an entire classroom. Immediately the teacher can involve his listeners in a tale of long ago or once upon a time. He can take child after child to places they could not possibly read about. He can jolt senses, stir imaginations, and provide young audiences with the literary heritage they so greatly deserve.

Storytelling is difficult—much more so than reading aloud. Storytelling techniques must be mastered if a teacher is going to be effective. But once they are, rewards are paid off in contagious excitement, expressive faces, and cries of "Tell it over! Tell it again!" To help the beginning storyteller, here are ten guides to good storytelling:[3]

1. Read story silently until you are familiar with the action sequence.
2. Read story aloud; listen to your voice.
3. Oral practice effectively brings to light weak spots in one's recollection of the story.
4. Enunciate clearly in a well-modulated voice.
5. Vary tone and pitch to animate the story.
6. The voice must display warmth, verve, and enthusiasm.
7. Practice before a mirror. Study facial expression and gestures.
8. Mimicry is an effective artifice in telling stories. Use it only if you have special aptitude.
9. Tell the story without any interruption. Explanations should be anticipated in advance and inserted in such a way as not to interrupt the action of the story.
10. Choose stories for your repertoire that you like to tell.

For better understanding of and appreciation for Indian cultures and the changes that are taking place in them, Indian children on the reservations are encour-

---

3. Victoria S. Johnson, "Windows on the World: Let's Tell More Stories," *Elementary English*, February 1968, pp. 259-260.

aged and helped to search out and read or tell stories and legends from their own and other tribes. Teachers also encourage children to invite tribal leaders or tribal citizens to come to school and tell stories and legends. When agreeable to the storytellers, the sessions are taped for future use.

Such programs can be developed with other disadvantaged groups of children. The Appalachian region is filled with American folklore. An excellent volume, *American Negro Folktales* (Fawcett, 1967), collected by Richard M. Dorson, is filled with wonderful tales teachers can tell their classes.

If children frequently hear many of the rich tales that are available, they will be more apt to run to books to find more and more.

Building Classroom Libraries

The classroom library can be the most important part of the learning environment when it contains books that meet the interests and needs of each individual child. And who knows such interests and needs better than the classroom teachers?

There are many ways to set up a classroom library; with a little effort, an exciting reading center can be developed. In one school where there was a lack of shelving, several teachers, with their students, set up a rolling library table. Books were placed on the table, which could be rolled around to the different rooms to service individuals or groups of children. Books were changed frequently by a committee of children who served as the roving librarians. This same technique can be employed in a single classroom utilizing a table-on-wheels to highlight special topics or themes such as Island Homes, Books in Spanish, Great Tastes in Literature, Poetry Parades, or Award Winning Books.

In classrooms where there is space available, a reading corner can be planned. Besides the books, a table and chair may be in the corner, and a rug or pillows placed on the floor for comfort while browsing or relaxing. Artifacts might "advertise" a specific book; for example, a cricket cage next to *The Cricket in Times Square,* a toy frog next to *Frog Went-a-Courtin',* or a kite next to *Mei Lei.*

Records of books read should appear somewhere in the classroom. One fourth-grade teacher utilizes a long piece of wood covered with brightly covered burlap as a House of Books. Each child has an envelope with his name printed on it, and when he finishes a book, he places an index card into the envelope listing the title, author, and a sentence or two about his reactions. This provides a quick check for both teachers and children of books read.

Another idea used to decorate an Appalachian classroom was the construction of book scrolls. Children decorated long pieces of brown wrapping paper and titled their scrolls "Sally's Book List," "Marilou's Memories," or "Jay Donald's Inventory." The scrolls were hung around the room, and each time a child completed a book, he added its title to his list along with a one-sentence summary and/or an illustration.

In a classroom where the population was entirely

Spanish-speaking, a teacher worked out a classroom library program that included only a few books at a time. The books were listed in a column on a large chart; the children's names were written across the top. Boys and girls were encouraged to rate the books by color—blue for excellent, yellow for fair, green for good, or purple for poor. When several opinions appeared, the teacher discussed the books with the entire class. Those volumes that received favorable reviews were kept on the shelf; those the children did not enjoy were removed and replaced with new titles.

If children are encouraged to have a say as to what goes into *their* libraries, more interest will be shown, and more reading and sharing of books will take place.

The Paperback Revolution

Paperback books have aided in building classroom libraries, and their popularity has become a twentieth-century phenomenon. They have contributed enormously to educational programs, particularly with disadvantaged youth. The low cost of paperbacks makes it easier to meet the individual needs of children who have infinite varieties of interests. Children who cannot afford to own hardcover volumes or children who do not have bookshops (or public libraries in their immediate vicinity) have benefited from classroom book clubs organized in schools.

The paperbacks published by Scholastic Book Services, Inc., are perhaps the most widely used in schools throughout the country. The company has five book clubs that service millions of children from kindergarten through twelfth grade. The clubs include: See-Saw Books (K-1), Lucky Book Club (2-3), Arrow Book Club (4-5-6), Teen Age Book Club (7-8-9), and Campus Book Club (10-11-12). Hundreds of titles, including paperback editions of children's books in the Initial Teaching Alphabet (i.t.a.), are available in high quality paperback editions. To obtain the free starter kits available for each club, write Scholastic at 904 Sylvan Avenue, Englewood Cliffs, New Jersey 07632.

The Viking Seafarer Books is a new series of quality paperback picture books for the very young and story books for the 8-12 year-old. The books priced at 65¢ and 75¢ include those created by top authors and illustrators in the field, such as Ludwig Bemelmans, Robert Mc-Closkey, Marie Hall Ets, and Rumer Godden. A catalog can be obtained from The Viking Press, Inc., 625 Madison Avenue, New York, New York 10022.

Dell Publishing Company, Inc., has also recently begun publishing high quality paperbound reprints for elementary school children. Yearling books are designed for grades two through eight and include books by such distinguished authors as Lois Lenski, E. B. White, Elizabeth Enright, and Pearl S. Buck; the Mayflower series contain contemporary fiction and nonfiction written for young people in grades six through nine; the Laurel-Leaf Library, appropriate for upper-elementary school students, includes classic collections of short stories and widely accepted contemporary books. A catalog describing the total program is available from the publisher, 750 Third Avenue, New York, New York 10017.

Doubleday & Company, Inc., has recently produced Zenith books, which are available in both a clothbound edition at $2.95 and a paperback edition at $1.45. Zenith books are designed "to encourage the slow, the bored, the inhibited student toward greater participation in the class. At the same time, their use will give all students a more balanced picture of American growth and development based on the achievements of America's minority citizens." Most of the titles in this series relate to Negro and Puerto Rican leaders. The texts are geared to the upper-elementary grades and have been approved for class use by the New York City, Los Angeles, Chicago, Boston, Philadelphia, Baltimore, and Washington, D. C., school systems. Additional information can be obtained by writing to Doubleday at Garden City, Long Island, New York 11531.

To find out about other companies that publish paperbacks for children, see the special supplement on paperbacks that appeared in *The New York Times Book Review*, Section 7, Part 2, on February 25, 1968.

Paperback bookshops are increasing in popularity in schools throughout the country and are operated by Parent-Teacher Associations, groups of children within the school, or by teachers. Such shops can meet the following needs: children can find a greater range of reading material and can have a variety of books to select from, read, and own; teachers can suggest various titles to augment the school curriculum; and parents have the opportunity to buy quality books for their children.

In one area where children cannot afford to buy paperbacks, a group of parents have set up a unique buying plan called "Save for a Book." Children from the various grades come three times a week to an area of the school library where the bookshop is housed. Each one is given a charge card on which is recorded how much money he has saved. Pennies, nickels, dimes, and quarters are given to the parents in charge, who keep records of the children's money. When a child has saved enough, he selects a book, hands in his charge card, and receives a new one.

This idea has worked effectively and has made it possible to put hundreds of books into hundreds of children's lives. Many of these children might never have had the opportunity to secure their own books if it were not for this plan. Paperbacks are a boon to reading programs for their cost is just right in a world where hardcover books are priced too high for the too many.

School and Public Libraries

The old image of the quiet, stuffy library is beginning to disappear. The concern today is to entice children into the library and provide activities that will be stimulating and exciting and make them want to come to the library frequently. A good example of this lively new approach is summed up by a one-page notice that appeared in the June 23, 1967, issue of *Top of the News,* p. 359, a journal published by the Young Adult Services and Children's Services Divisions of the American Library Association (see opposite page).

SUMMER SEASONING

WHAT? STORY PICNICS—
      sandwiches
      milk
      apples
      stories

WHERE? INNER-CITY BRANCH LIBRARIES
      on the lawn
      on the steps
      in the community room
      even in the children's room

WHY? TO DRAW OUR CHILDREN TO US
      everybody loves a picnic
      many children need lunch
      summer should be fun

BUT! *We do not eat at the library.*
Everybody knows we do not eat at the library.
WHY NOT EAT AT THE LIBRARY?

BUT! *Crumbs. Sticky fingers. Petals all over the place.*
BROOMS. PAPER NAPKINS.
WASHROOM PARADES.

BUT! *Libraries are for books. Not for free lunches.*
LIBRARIES ARE FOR PEOPLE.
LIBRARIES ARE TO LEAD CHILDREN TO BOOKS.

BUT! *Even if picnics would bring our children to us—who*
would do the peanut-butter-and-jelly part?

TEENAGE VOLUNTEERS
   FROM THE INNER-CITY BRANCH
   FROM COOPERATING OUTER BRANCHES
Suburban youngsters look for inner-city summer
service jobs. Include supper-picnic programs for
teenagers from city and suburbs.

We look for ways to interest the young in becoming librarians.
Give them, this summer, a chance to know the challenges and
satisfactions of library service to inner-city children.
WHAT CAN WE POSSIBLY LOSE BY TRYING?

School libraries are usually established to meet curriculum needs of children and teachers and are used by groups more often than by individuals. Public libraries, on the other hand, are more comprehensive and try to make books of all kinds available to everyone. Public libraries provide many services for parents, teachers, and children. Even in many small towns, collections of art prints and records are circulated, storytelling programs are held, and foreign language book and record collections are made available. Library lessons and tours for special groups can usually be arranged. In rural areas bookmobiles, libraries that travel through communities containing rather complete collections of adult and children's books, are quite common.

Local newspapers are good sources to check for special library programs. For example, *The Cleveland Press* advertised its Fifteenth Annual Book Fair in the fall of 1967, which was held at The Cleveland Public Library. Twenty-nine authors and artists were invited to talk about their books and perform fascinating chalk talks. During the week noted personalities appeared, including Hardie Gramatky, creator of *Little Toot*, Brian Wildsmith, author-illustrator of many texts for young children, Mary O'Neill, the poet, and Charlemae Hill Rollins, author of books about Negro history and culture.

Since 1960 an annual book fair has been held in Washington, D. C. An elementary school in New York City holds an annual book fair on November 19, Puerto Rico Discovery Day. It features books and material published by the Instituto de Cultura de Puerto Rico for parents, teachers, and students.

When school and public libraries cooperate, they can provide the key to opening library doors to children in all areas. Every child should be encouraged to obtain a library card—and use it. The many activities held in the library and frequent visits to libraries can be valuable additional incentives for reading.

Learning About Authors

It is always surprising to hear concepts that children have about authors of books. Time and time again children utter statements such as:

Do authors sleep?

I thought all authors were dead!

People who write books must be strange.

Where do people who write books get their names from?

Do people who write books live in regular houses or in publishing houses?

If children are fed facts and anecdotes about the lives of authors, such misconceptions will disappear. There are many ways to acquaint children with authors. *The Junior Book of Authors* (edited by Kunitz and Haycraft, Wilson, 1951) and *More Junior Authors* (edited by Muriel Fuller, Wilson, 1963) provide hundreds of short autobiographical and biographical sketches of reknown personalities in the field of children's literature. Another excellent volume is *Tellers of Tales: Children's Books and Their Authors from 1800-1964* (Watts, 1965). Included in this reference book are many biographies of popular English authors such as P. L. Travers, A. A.

Milne, and Hugh Lofting. These volumes can be found in most children's rooms of public libraries.

Many publishing houses also provide fact sheets about their authors' lives and will send material for classroom use. Various trade journals and popular magazines often feature interviews or articles about authors. Typical information to share with children is:

> Dr. Seuss' real name is T. S. Geisel. . . . At least eight million Seuss books have been sold since the first one, *And to Think that I Saw It on Mulberry Street,* (which) was enthusiastically rejected by 26 publishing houses.[4]

> Mariana Prieto was born in Cincinnati, Ohio, but her family moved to Cuba when she was six months old. She spoke English and Spanish.[5]

> In an autobiographical sketch Herbert S. Zim relates: "My room at home overflowed with plants, growing and pressed; several aquaria; boxes of rocks; and cages of toads, salamanders, and snakes.[6]

Writing letters to authors is a stimulating way for children to obtain information. Children can write to authors in care of their publishing houses and will usually receive replies. Virginia Lee Burton, Caldecott Award winner, received many letters from young readers. She stated:

---

4. Arthur Godron. "The Wonderful Wizard of Soledad Hill," *Woman's Day,* September 1964, pp. 74+.
5. Irene Buckley. "Mariana Prieto: She Has Something to Say," *Elementary English,* January 1967, pp. 7-11.
6. Stanley J. Kunitz and Howard Haycraft. *The Junior Book of Authors,* 2nd rev. ed. New York: H. W. Wilson Company, 1951, pp. 307.

I spend a great deal of time answering them personally and also make a sketch from the book they are writing about. Recently I heard from the teacher of a little boy who was not interested in learning to read. After my letter he changed and became an avid reader.[7]

A sixth-grade class was inspired to write to author George Selden after its teacher had read *The Cricket in Times Square* (Farrar, 1960), runner-up for the 1960 Newbery Award. Several weeks after the class letters were mailed, the following reply came:

> I have just spent a delightful and flattering half-hour reading all your letters, and truly I don't know how to thank you! I enjoyed every one of them, and I know I should have taken the time to answer each one individually. But I have just finished the first draft of a novel I'm writing—for adults this time—and frankly, I am so exhausted that I hope this one note to all of you will be sufficient.
>
> Your encouragement is heartwarming! I would like very much to write a sequel to *The Cricket*—along the lines you suggest—and I think some day I will, if I can ever find the time!
>
> Several of you asked whether I have had any other books published. Well, I have. *The Dog that Could Swim Under Water* and *The Garden Under the Sea*. Both were released by The Viking Press. The first is about a dog I owned when I was a child, and the second is about a fish, a crab, a lobster, and a starfish that live together at the bottom of Long Island Sound.
>
> Thank you all again.[8]

7. Paul C. Burns and Ruth Hines. "Virginia Lee Burton," *Elementary English,* April 1967, pp. 331-5.
8. Used by permission of George Selden.

Needless to say, every child in the room was ecstatic over this treasure, and the public library was bombarded with requests for the books mentioned in Mr. Selden's letter.

A second letter, written by a fourth-grade class, invited Tillie S. Pine, co-author of many nonfiction books for children, to visit their class. She accepted and presented a lively lecture to the youngsters on how her books grew from their conception to the day of publication. The children responded with letters to thank her for her visit.

An Author's Afternoon is an exciting event for children to plan and participate in. One such affair was held in Harlem. The authors asked to visit were ones who wrote books about minority children: Ezra Jack Keats, Ellen Tarry, Ruth Sonneborn, Brinton Turkle, and Pura Belpré White. Educators, parents, and children representing School District #4 were invited to attend the function. The Viking Press made books available at a 40 percent discount so that many children could purchase copies.

The authors discussed their lives and their books. Hearing Keats talk about Peter, the main character in *The Snowy Day,* as being himself as a small child, listening to Ellen Tarry discussing the highpoints and the pitfalls of researching her recent biography *Young Jim: The Story of James Weldon Johnson* (Dodd, Mead, 1967), and seeing Pura Belpré White conduct a spontaneous puppet show were instant reading incentives. After a panel presentation and a question-answer session, the authors mingled with the children over juice and cookies and autographed their works.

Such an opportunity is rare in the lives of most children; however, such events can be planned in any area of the country. The Children's Book Council, 175 Fifth Avenue, New York, New York 10010, offers speakers' lists of authors and artists who are willing to speak to various groups—some for fees and others for merely the payment of transportation costs. The lists are compiled by state and are available free if a large, self-stamped addressed envelope is enclosed. Publishing houses, local libraries, reading groups, and educational organizations can also be of great aid in arranging an Author's Afternoon.

Sharing Literature Through Experiences

Literature can be shared in many ways. The experiences provided, however, should be meaningful ones —ones children enjoy taking part in and which grow naturally from their love of books. Forced book reports telling "the part I like best" or "what the book means to me" can be terribly dull. The disadvantaged child is most often one who is nonverbal; therefore, it is of utmost importance not to limit him to written book reports. Children can love a book without analyzing it to death or without always writing about it. The written book report is a rather closed street of communication— the child writes something, the teacher reads it, and that is usually the end. For a child to finish such books as *The Two Giants* (Pantheon, 1967) or *Potates, Potatoes* (Harper, 1967) and write "the book is about . . ." or "the part I liked best is . . ." is a tragic waste. It is like going to a garden of magnificent flowers and smelling only one or going to a circus to look at only one ring!

There are many ways to encourage the sharing of literature and many reasons to do so. For the disadvantaged child such opportunities can:

- Provide an avenue through which he can relate his personal feelings.
- Aid in developing his creative potential.
- Show concrete evidence of his ability and show that he can produce a successfully completed project.
- Provide exposure to new media and new ways of thinking about books.

The more opportunities the child has to be creative, the more he will create. Provide children with new experiences such as the following activities, give them the chance to discover their abilities, stand aside—and let them grow!

Mapping Books

Maps of a city, state, continent, or of the world can be posted in the classroom to pinpoint places where stories in children's literature occurred. Pins with strings attached can show, for example, Wisconsin, where *Caddie Woodlawn* takes place; San Francisco, where two pigeons built a nest in a huge letter of a neon sign in Don Freeman's, *Fly High, Fly Low*; or India, where Raman in *What Then, Raman* lived. Perhaps a state where someone in a biography lived or died might be highlighted. Where fictitious places are key points in books, have the class members create original maps. Encourage them to let their imaginations soar as they map out the Yellow Brick Road in *The Wizard of Oz*, or *Rabbit Hill*, for nowhere will they find such places on a conventional map.

Literature Newsletter

A bulletin board can be utilized to develop a Literature Newsletter modeled after a newspaper. Children can decide what columns or features they would like on the board, and a rotating editorial staff can periodically change the news. This device is a good one for highlighting interesting events in books. After reading a book, a child can write a brief statement about a character or event and give it to the proper editor. A headline might read:

MAX RETURNS
From *Where the Wild Things Are*

A lost and found item or a society note might be given to the feature editor:

LOST AND FOUND
Dog Lost. Reward. Contact Juanito in *My Dog Is Lost*.

SOCIETY COLUMN
Mr. March returned from the Civil War. Jo, Beth, Amy, and Meg, his daughters, planned welcome home party.

A sports item would be handed to the sports editor:

JACKIE ROBINSON SIGNED
TO WORLD FAMOUS CLUB

News items can be illustrated and/or book jackets can accompany the stories. A literature bulletin board provides the child a method of reviewing books frequently, easily, and creatively.

Instant Reaction Card File

Children can be encouraged to record their instant reactions to books read on index cards. A young child or a child who has difficulty writing can *tell* the teacher what he thinks about a book. The teacher, acting as scribe, can write down his comments. Other children can write their own reactions to books they read. These cards can be filed in a small box and can, at a glance, tell the teacher the types of books the children are reading and how many books they have completed. In this way over-structured book reports can be avoided, and the time usually spent on the preparation of them can be used for more creative ways of sharing literature. The samples below show two children's instant reactions:

> I read *Straight Hair, Curly Hair* (Crowell, 1966) and I liked it because I never knew anything about hair and I was amazed to find out all the things you can do with hair and I did them. And I know why my hair is curly, not straight, now.
>
> *Third-grader*

> *The Story of My Life* (Doubleday, 1954) by Helen Keller is the most beautiful book I have ever read. Even when I think about Helen's life, I get goose flesh bumps. I loved the book, and I loved the way it was written. I am going to read it again this summer.
>
> *Sixth-grader*

What more could be said or how much better could

they have expressed themselves if the children who wrote the above had worked—even additional minutes— on these reports?

Descriptive Passage Portals

An effective technique used in several schools is a Descriptive Passage Portal. Teachers place a large brown envelope near the door and encourage children to contribute cards on which they have written favorite passages from their readings. When the children line up for gym period, to walk to the auditorium for a special event, or to go home at the close of the school day, a child is selected to reach in and read (or have the teacher read) a passage submitted by a student:

> Far down the road she heard the pound, pound, pound of horses' hoofs. She stood still, undecided. Should she hide in the woods? She gathered up her long skirt in one hand, preparing to run. She wouldn't run. Her skirt would be snagged and torn by briars, she might trip and fall. Besides, she still did not know how she was going to get Old Rit and Ben to the North. She might have to take them on a train, and she couldn't ride on a train with her clothing torn, it was one of the earmarks of a fugitive.
>
> • • •
>
> The barn was very large. It was very old. It smelled of hay and it smelled of manure. It smelled of the perspiration of tired horses and the wonderful sweet breath of patient cows. It often had the sort of peaceful smell—as though nothing bad could happen ever again in the world.

The above passages from *Harriet Tubman, Conductor of the Underground Railway* by Ann Petry (Crowell,

1955) and *Charlotte's Web* by E. B. White (Harper, 1952) take only seconds to read. They provide children with ideas for the-book-to-take-next from the library shelf and give them a wonderful feeling of pride and satisfaction when *their* descriptive passage is read before passing through the portal.

Turning Books into Art Experiences

Books can be shared through a variety of art experiences. Individuals, groups of children, or a whole class can prepare collages or murals. Large, brown wrapping paper can be used as a background, and a variety of materials can be attached to it. The specific theme of a collage or mural should be decided upon by the class. One fourth-grade decided to depict the tea party scene from *Alice In Wonderland* and made a long, six-foot mural. Alice, the Mad Hatter, and the March Hare were blown-up to giant proportions; cloth was used for clothing, colored yarn for hair, and plastic toy dishes for the table setting; the background was painted in tempera, and the finished product was placed in the school hall for all the students to thoroughly enjoy.

Younger children could depict scenes from their favorite books on burlap. Characters and objects cut from paper and/or material can be applied to the burlap with thread or glue.

Constructing puppets of favorite book characters is another way of sharing literature. Children on every grade level can produce various types of puppets with great satisfaction. Simple drawings can be stapled to sticks or tongue depressors to obtain interesting effects. Large corks can easily be turned into puppets by using thumbtacks for eyes, yarn for hair, and paper for noses and mouths. Sticks can be used and inserted into the base of the cork for movement. Original drawings can also be made and thumb-tacked onto corks.

Papier mâché, potatoes, paper bags, and socks are other items that can be used for puppet construction. There are many books on the art, history, and the making of puppets, including:

Baird, Bil. *The Art of the Puppet.* New York: Macmillan, 1965.
The famous puppeteer presents a world-wide survey of puppetry from earliest times to the present day.

Cummings, Richard. *101 Hand Puppets.* New York: David Mckay Company, 1962.
101 easily made puppets are described in this text for young readers.

Pels, Gertrude. *Easy Puppets: Making and Using Hand Puppets.* New York: Crowell, 1951.
Directions are given for making unusual puppets from such things as carrots, soda-straws, and rubber balls.

Philpott, A. R. *Let's Look at Puppets.* Chicago: A. Whitman, 1967.
An excellent text for young children describing how puppets are used and made in such places as Africa, Spain, Mexico, South America, and Viet Nam.

Puppets provide an excellent outlet for encouraging more effective speech. Children who are shy or who cannot speak English fluently often find it easier to speak through a puppet, for it is not they who are talking but the character whom the puppet represents.

Original book jackets can spark a great deal of creativity. Children can design their own jackets and display them next to the original ones designed by the publishing houses. They can also write an advertisement, a summary of the book, or a biographical sketch of the author inside the jacket.

With the wide use of overhead projectors in schools today, child-made transparencies are good media for sharing literature. In one fifth-grade classroom a child chose the classic Puerto Rican folktale *Perez and Martina* and read his classmates the tale. Various children volunteered to draw scenes from the book without seeing the original drawings. Boys and girls drew Señor Perez, Señorita Martina, Señor Cock, and Señor Cricket. After several days, when the drawings were finished the child read the book again, this time showing on the overhead projector the drawings the children had made on transparencies. Then the text's original illustrations were shown for comparison.

Table displays are popular devices used to share books. Simple backgrounds can be made and three dimensional objects can be placed in front of them to highlight scenes from books.

Mobiles can be designed by individuals or groups. Cutouts or realia tied to strings and balanced from a wire hangar can make very successful literary displays.

Children's books, imagination, and simple materials can be combined to offer all children exciting and worthwhile experiences and can provide the transportation to journey after journey to the land of literature.

For Further Reading

Arbuthnot, May Hill. *Children and Books,* rev. ed. Chicago: Scott, Foresman, 1964.
An excellent reference book for parents, teachers, and librarians. The text covers the realm of literature from Mother Goose to present day trade books.

Brown, Harriet B., and Sinnette, Elinor D. "The School Library Program in a Depressed Area," *A.L.A. Bulletin,* July-August 1964, pp. 643–7.
A New York City-wide library program is discussed.

"Finding the Right Book," *The Instructor,* November 1966, Library Supplement.
Ten articles appear on selecting books for the library. Of special interest are the articles by Effie Lee Morris, "Choosing Books for the Deprived," and Ruth Hadlock's "'Specially Good for the Deprived."

Haviland, Virginia. *Children's Literature: A Guide to Reference Sources.* Washington, D.C.: Library of Congress, 1966.
An excellent annotated bibliography describing "books, articles, and pamphlets selected on the basis of their estimated usefulness to adults concerned with the creation, reading, or study of children's books."

Hopkins, Lee Bennett. "Did You Know that Books Are by People?" *Today's Catholic Teacher,* May 3, 1968, pp. 27, 44–5.
Ideas to acquaint children with the people behind the books—from authors to printers.

———. "Negro Life in Current American Children's Literature," *Bookbird,* March 1968, pp. 12–16.
A review of current books published in the United States which truly reflect the Negro in the 1960's.

————, and Shapiro, Annette Frank. "Pupil Teachers," *The Reading Teacher,* November 1967, pp. 128–9.

An article describing a story reading service set up in a Harlem school, one which deepens and enriches the life of the "pupil-teacher" as well as the children to whom he reads.

Huck, Charlotte S., and Kuhn, Doris Young. *Children's Literature in the Elementary School,* 2nd ed. New York: Holt, Rinehart and Winston, 1968.

An excellent reference and source book for the teacher, librarian, and parent. This text discusses the entire realm of children's literature.

Hürlimann, Bettina. *Three Centuries of Children's Books in Europe.* Cleveland: World Publishing Co., 1968.

The history of children's books is scholarly traced in Europe from Aesop's *Fables* and *Pinocchio* up through more recent classics as *Babar the Elephant.* An excellent volume, giving a rounded picture of children's literature from nursery rhymes to politics in books for children. Many fine prints, both in black and white and in color, as well as photographs.

Joseph, Sister Frances. "Children's Literature: Springboard to Interest," *Catholic School Journal,* October 1967, pp. 57–8.

Ideas on how teachers can bring literature and children together.

Nora, Sister Mary, and French, Ruth. "What are Some Resources for the Teacher of Children's Literature?" *Elementary English,* May 1964, pp. 516–25+.

A selective, annotated sampling of books, motion pictures, records, and films is given for the elementary school teacher's use. Most of this issue is devoted to children's literature and contains other informative articles.

Pellowski, Anne. *The World of Children's Literature.* New York: R. R. Bowker, 1968.

An expensive volume ($18.75) which lists more than 4,400 entries of books for children. The author-title-subject index contains over 15,000 listings. This is the first international bibliography on children's literature and libraries and is a useful tool to anyone working with or concerned about books.

Sawyer, Ruth. *The Way of the Storyteller*. New York: Viking, 1945; Compass Books, paper, 1962.

Besides giving a history of storytelling and techniques to use with children, the author includes 11 stories for telling, plus reading and story lists.

Thornley, Gwendolyn. "Storytelling Is Fairy Gold," *Elementary English*, January 1968, pp. 67–79.

An article based on Ruth Sawyer's statement that "the world would be a dreary place were there no passing of fairy gold." It lists a comprehensive selection of stories to tell children from two-years-old through to the teens.

Experiences with Written Expression
"Am I A Author Now?"

CHILDREN'S WRITING must stem directly from common events that occur in the classroom or from experiences that are a part of their personal lives. These experiences can be real or imaginary, but they must be the child's own. Children living in disadvantaged areas are often much less interested in writing than they are in reading. Many times they feel that they have nothing to say or nothing to write about. The classroom teacher must constantly utilize a variety of devices and techniques that can provide content for written expression. A local field trip, an area of the social studies, a science activity, viewing a film, and listening to a live or recorded program are common group experiences that can motivate writing.

Today children come to school with a great diversity of culture, customs, and mores. This can pose a problem for the classroom teacher; on the other hand it provides a constant source of new ideas and raw material with which to experiment. For instance, one teacher whose class was 50 percent Negro and 50 percent Spanish used an effective bulletin board display to alleviate resentment between the groups in her third-grade class. The title of her bulletin board read

IN SPANISH **FOOD** IS **COMIDAS!**

Two lists appeared on the bulletin board; one showed Spanish words, the other showed their English translations:

frutas	is	fruit
sopa	is	soup
carnes	is	meat
cafe	is	coffee
leche	is	milk
manzana	is	apple

Both Spanish and Negro children gained better knowledge of one another's language, and soon simple statements and stories were created in English and Spanish on experience charts.

Experience charts are excellent devices for making children interested in writing. The use of such charts is quite common in the primary grades, and the values gained from recording children's experiences on chart paper or on the chalkboard are immeasurable. The greatest advantage of making experience charts is that it is a cooperative process. The child speaks his language to the teacher, the teacher writes it down exactly as it was dictated, and the child knows that it is *his*.

This technique should be used on every elementary grade level, particularly with the child for whom English is a second language. In Public School 108, in Manhattan, Nancy Bauer works with Spanish-speaking children and uses the following technique for vocabularly development and creative story writing. A child is given a piece of oak tag on which to draw a picture. When the picture is completed, she works with the child on a one-to-one basis asking: "What does your picture *say?* What's this *about?*" The child dictates his story for her to write. He then chooses a title for the story which she prints on another piece of oak tag. The pages are then fastened together, and the child has a book!

An interesting extension of this project is that the teacher asks the child to select from his story the words that are new or hard for him to recognize. These words are printed on cards and placed in an envelope attached to the back cover of his book. A second set of cards is also made, which is given to the child to take home to learn.

Medalia dictated:

My Grandmother
My grandmother is hurting my sister because she doesn't want to come upstairs to the house.

The words she selected were *hurting, doesn't,* and *house.*

Jose dictated:

The Witch
The witch is flying in the air. She takes boys who don't sleep.

The words he selected to learn were *witch* and *flying.*

Lessons such as these enable the child to be more fluent in his expression and free him from the physical mechanics of writing. Children need this freedom, and they need to feel confident in creative expression before they can actually learn to write for themselves.

Written expression provides the child with a deep satisfaction of being able to communicate values, needs, and emotional outlets. A fifth-grade child wrote:

> I feel so bad today. My ma had to go to work and was afraid to leave me alone in the apartment. Last night police were all over the place looking for someone with a gun. I wasn't afraid though. I told my ma how I could take care of myself. She felt better and went to work.

A sixth-grade child expressed the following about his neighborhood:

> My block stinks! It has cans and cans and cans all over the place and garbage and rats and ugly people always asken for monee. If the city would only clean up the place maybe the people would clean themselves up and become human beens.

During the Christmas season a fifth-grade boy created this poem:

> 'Twas the night before Christmas
> And all through the house
> Everyone was stirring, even the mouse.
> The stockings were hung by the incinerator
> In hope that the heat would come sooner or later.

An eleven-year-old child paraphrased the Twenty-Third Psalm:

The Lord is my probation officer.
He will help me.
He tries to help me make it every day.
He makes me play it cool.[1]

Children will only create and reveal their inner
thoughts to a teacher who will accept them for what
they are. When children write like this—when they
create from their hearts—it is useless to take a red pencil
from the desk drawer and correct spelling errors or
misuse of grammar and punctuation. If the teacher attempts this, he will not obtain creative responses the
next time round; inner thoughts will be kept inside, and
deep feelings will be turned into superficial sentences.
The idea of assigning one title to an entire class, such as
"What I Did on My Summer Vacation," or "My Best
Experience," or "Fire Prevention Week and What It
Means to Me," is outdated and horribly dull!

Recently a fourth-grade teacher asked her class to
write on the topic "Here Comes the Snow!" She felt this
was an excellent topic since it was a cold, wintry day
and the first snowfall of the year had just started. She
distributed paper, gave last minute directions, and told
the children: "Write creatively now. You have 15 minutes!" Several minutes went by. Suddenly the teacher
looked up and saw Yael shaking and crying uncontrol-
lably. She took Yael out of the room and calmed her.

"What is the matter, Yael?" she asked.

The reply was: "I can't write about that stuff. The
world is coming to an end! I'm afraid."

Yael was from Israel and had never seen snow before!

1. Reverend Carl F. Burke, "Rephrasing Makes Bible Meaningful to
Children from Urban Slums," *Today's Child,* May 1965.

The remainder of the class compositions were not half as exciting as the fast falling snow outside. In the same school—just doors down the hall—a second-grader remarked to his teacher: "Ya' know what it looks like? It looks like someone havin' a pillow-fight."

In Intermediate School 88, in New York City, Margaret Vranesh, a sixth-seventh grade teacher who does a great deal with language arts and social studies, encouraged her class to write their thoughts and feelings after the assassination of Dr. Martin Luther King, Jr. The children in the Harlem area came to school the day after Dr. King was murdered in Memphis feeling tense, keyed-up, and frightened over the tragic occurrence. Creative expression helped them to readjust their thinking and to let off steam. Sixth-grade girls wrote:

> When President Kennedy died I was about eight years old, but I did not know what really happened. But I could feel the tenseness of the whole house. But I really didn't understand. But now I know the pain to lose someone you believed in. If Mr. King was a relative I couldn't have felt any more heartbroken.

> Mr. King we will never be able to forget you. We will love you and remember you in our heart. For it will be peace on earth for remembering you. In our heart will be peace alone.

> When I found out that he was shot I could not believe it. I was hoping he would not die! But a little while later they said he was dead! My brother ran in the house and said there is a riot on 125th street and stores were broken into.

And a sixth grade boy stated:

> I cried like a baby when I was looking at TV. It was so sad.

Many children are not as fluent or expressive as those whose work is cited above. Writing is often painful for children, and there are some who just cannot put their thoughts into writing. Exercises in brief writing experiences can sometimes pave the way for longer writing activities. If teachers begin with techniques that are within the child's grasp and allow for a sense of completion and accomplishment, children will progress to the more mature forms of written expression.

The techniques that follow cite several writing experiences that have been tried and tested in disadvantaged areas—and have worked!

Quick Accomplishment Ideas

Using the Alphabet

A lack of vocabulary is both a handicap and a problem for the child who tries to record his thoughts and feelings in writing. The use of the ABC's has proven to be very successful on every grade level. One teacher whose class was studying Africa assigned letters to individual children. They in turn researched books and encyclopedias to find words to match their respective letters. Words were then placed on oak tag charts and tacked around the room:

> A is for African animals
> B is for bronze figures
> C is for crops.

Another teacher used this same idea for a science unit on rocks and obtained results such as:

A is for albite
B is for bituminous
C is for calcite.

Projects can also include making booklets or combining other forms of writing on charts, for example, poetry forms, riddles, or similes.

The ABC sticklers, such as Q, X, and Z, sometimes pose problems: however, careful research on the part of the children might reveal some surprises. When a fifth-grade class prepared a project on the Westward Movement, one child was stumped on the letter Q for several days. He finally found "Q is for quince," which led to a very dramatic quince-and-cracker tasting party. The letter X can always be the unknown, and Z gives everyone trouble. An anecdote that is fun to share with children is that even the Bell Telephone Company had trouble with Q and Z—they left them off the telephone dial! This usually sends youngsters home to check to see if the teacher is right—and they will find out that he is!

The use of the ABC's was used differently in a fifth-grade classroom. The teacher selected one word pertaining to a unit of study and had the children find a word or phrase using the initial letter. For example, the word PEACE was used while studying the United Nations and motivated one student to write:

P is for **people**—all the people in the world.
E is for **eager** to help.
A is for **all** the countries that belong to the United Nations.
C is for the **councils** which makes up the UN.
E is for **everlasting** peace!

Similes

Similes are figures of speech that are direct comparisons, using *like* or *as*. Provide children with several phrases such as "As white as . . ." or "As green as . . ." Immediate responses will probably be "As white as snow" and "As green as grass!" Many teachers become discouraged when children come up with such ordinary responses, yet what better examples are there? After discussing word comparisons and word imagery, allow the children to select their own words and look for unusual and exciting phrases. Examples from fourth-grade children in Newark, New Jersey, included:

> As white as the new paint on my kitchen wall.
> As green as my father's eyes.
> As fluffy as the featheriest feather.
> As cold as death.

Definitions via Charlie Brown

Charles M. Schulz's Peanuts characters—Charlie and Sally Brown, Lucy and Linus Von Pelt, and Snoopy—have opened up an entire world of creative writing activities for elementary school children. Books such as *Happiness Is a Warm Puppy* (United Feature, 1962), *Security Is a Thumb and Blanket* (United Feature, 1963), and *Love Is Walking Hand in Hand* (United Feature, 1965) have been used effectively on all grade levels to motivate young writers. One third-grade class experimented with "Misery is . . ." and came up with:

MISERY IS . . .
when there is a power failure and you have ice cream
in the freezer.
when a school holiday comes on a Saturday.
when your favorite magazine is at the dentist's and
you have no cavities.

This technique is short, spontaneous, and permits easy
success to even the slowest child in the class. A sixth-
grade girl created the following definition-poem:

FUN IS TO . . .
Fun is to play
    in some hay.
Fun is to beat my drums,
    while I'm munching crumbs.
Fun is to cook
    while reading a book.
Fun is to stop
    when I'm just on the top!

The Five Senses

Claudia Lewis states in *Writing for Children* (Simon
and Schuster, 1964) that a child's language is:

a language of action, of sensory images, a language
telling of the touch of things, and their colors, odors,
and sounds. It has movement, pace, rhythm. For the
child is not a static creature. Out of his reservoir of
sensory responsiveness come rushing up the words that
move with rhythm of this thought; galloping, bumping,
coasting, swinging words. How does the choppy sea
go? Why, "Wibbly, woobly, dabbly, dubbly, bibbly,"
of course . . . Rhythm of sounds, rhythm of movement,
these are one. . . .

Emphasizing the five senses in written expression can be utilized in many ways to develop the ability to keenly depict those things children see, hear, touch, taste and smell. Mary O'Neill in *Hailstones and Halibut Bones*[2] writes of various colors and how they evoke our senses. For example:

WHAT IS BROWN?

Brown is the color of a country road
Back of a turtle
Back of a toad.
Brown is cinnamon
And morning toast
And the smell of
The Sunday roast.
Brown is the color of work.
And the sound of a river,
Brown is bronze and a bow
And a quiver.
Brown is the house
On the edge of town
Where wind is tearing
The shingles down.
Brown is a freckle
Brown is a mole
Brown is the earth
When you dig a hole.
Brown is the hair
On many a head
Brown is chocolate

---

2. Mary O'Neill. *Hailstones and Halibut Bones*. New York: Double-day, 1961, pp. 23-4. An excellent sound, color film narrated by Celeste Holm is available, which combines the illustrations and the color with the reading of the poems.

And gingerbread.
Brown is a feeling
You get inside
When wondering makes
Your mind grow wide.
Brown is a leather shoe
And a good glove————
Brown is as comfortable
As love.

Children can be encouraged to write about colors that are not included in Miss O'Neill's book, or they can be freed to describe their own feelings and images of color.

An exciting project has been developed in Dayton, Ohio, under the direction of Martha Baines, art consultant for the Dayton schools. With the use of federal funds under Title I of ESEA, she has established a New Visions Museum:

> The museum deliberately takes into account the way each of the five senses contributes to the learning process and provides specific experiences for each. Younger children squeal with delight as they taste mysterious substances or smell unknown bottles—then discover the substances are things they've always known about. For the first time many of them are learning to *use* their senses as a means of knowing and understanding the world about them.[3]

A museum of this type could be easily set up within a classroom. This, plus the use of field trips and creative dramatics, may spark ideas for exploring and writing about the five senses.

---

3. "A Child's Museum of the Senses," *Grade Teacher*, May/June 1967, pp. 106-109+.

Pictures and realia can be used to motivate writing experiences. Pictures cut from inexpensive calendars, books, or magazines can be grouped around a theme or used for creating captions and titles or for writing descriptions. Placing illustrated material and/or realia under an opaque projector can dramatically produce results. Recently a group of fifth-graders wrote the following captions after viewing a picture of a young boy holding his report card in one hand and his dog in the other:

> I wish my dad could sign blindfolded!
>
> Oh, if I could only switch report cards for a day, then everything would be all right.
>
> Look, kid, I have my problems, too.
>
> Take two aspirins, that's what your mother does.
>
> Rover, I've got problems!

A sixth-grade class collected a variety of pictures of cats and created captions about them. A bulletin board display, in a main corridor of the school, entitled Creative Kittens generated howls of laughter from every grade in the building.

The power of observation can be developed for exciting, creative writing results. A group or a class can sit in front of a tree and look at it as they never looked before! They can describe another classmate in detail, write about things in the school or community they have lived with but perhaps never noticed such as the colors of street signs, the type of plant life growing between the cracks in the sidewalks, or the variety of building materials used in the construction of houses and stores.

No matter how depressed an area is, something of beauty can be found nearby if children are encouraged to look for it.

SOUND

Sounds can motivate interesting writing experiences. The word ONAMOTOPOEIA was placed on a chalkboard of a fourth-grade classroom and defined as a word that imitates the sound it describes. Children quickly responded with phrases such as the honking horn, the buzzing bee, crackling, crunchy cereal, rain's pitter patter, and the swish of a broom. Another fourth-grade class in a Harlem school composed the following poem after discussing noise:

NOISE

Noise, noise everywhere
What to do! It's always there.
Bang! Pow! Zoom! Crunch!
Buzz! Crack! Crack! Munch!

In the air, on the ground,
Noise, noise all around.
Dogs barking, cars parking,
Planes flying, babies crying.

Sh . . . sh . . . time for sleep
Not a single little peep.
Oh no—through the door—
Comes a noisy, awful snore.

Tick-tock—stop the clock.
Stop the yelling on my block
Close the windows, shut them tight
Cotton in ear . . . nighty-night

Sounds of the city's machines and people, sounds of the weather, and sounds heard in nature can all lead to many new exciting writing adventures. Experiment with:

Open the window and what do you hear?
What does night sound like?
Compare city sounds to country sounds.
What sound does the seashore make?
What sounds remind you of winter, summer, spring, fall?

Music can spark many activities. The sounds of various instruments, rhythmical beats, and the ways musical effects reflect various cultures and environments can be used in the classroom. Sid Mitchell, a creative, young teacher in Hartford, Connecticut, used a recording of "The William Tell Overture" with a group of disadvantaged children in a fifth-grade. The class discussed the record at great length after hearing it. The record was played again; this time the children were encouraged to jot down their feelings while listening to the music.

This music makes me feel like I'm in a symphony orchestra. I could hear the violin playing. It makes me feel like I'm in heaven. I feel like I have no problems (but, I do you know) in the world. Close to the end I could hear the flute go "Tweet, tweet, tweet, tweet," and the drums go "Boom, boom, boom, boom," and I could hear the Lone Ranger . . . I liked that part.

• • •

The Lark commercial! The burglar is dancing. He must be the cat burglar. What a queer cat burglar it is. Go man, go! The burglar has burned down a house! "Burn baby, burn!" The chase, they've captured him. His last words were, "Keep the faith, Baby!

TOUCH

In a first-grade room in Cleveland, Ohio, a touch box contained a variety of items such as sandpaper, different textured wood and cloth, paper clips, foam rubber, and plastics. Individual children took an item from the box and described what it felt like. Responses were recorded on a chart, and poems and stories were written from the vocabularly lists developed.

A nature table containing items representing different textures was set up in a New Jersey classroom. Children would go to the table and feel the items and then prepared charts with simple sentences and drawings. "A *coarse* rock," "A *silky* flower," "A *bumpy* twig," and "A *pimpled* gourd" are examples of second-graders' responses to nature's textures.

TASTE AND SMELL

A lesson to evoke responses to the senses of taste and smell was prepared in a kindergarten class. A display consisting of smelling bottles and tasting jars was set up. The children were asked to use their senses to guess what was in either the bottles or the jars. For example, the children had to determine between sugar and salt. Since they are both white in color, the children had to taste the contents in order to identify it.

In a fifth-grade room, candy canes were distributed to an entire class and the words TASTE and SMELL were printed on the chalkboard. As the children ate their candy canes, they called out words or phrases that described them. SIGHT, TOUCH, and SOUND were soon added to the list, which when finished read:

ABOUT THE CANDY CANE

TASTES	TOUCH
scrumptious	sticky
pepperminty	gooey
lousy	slippery
watery	rough
hot	smooth
spicy	flat
delicious	round
like chewing nuts	hard
like lipstick	lumpy
like something foreign	

SIGHT	SOUNDS
red	crunchy
like striped toothpaste	crispy
like a drill	noisy
like a barber pole	like chewing on ice
good to suck on	crackling
like candy	baby biting on a nipple
	like the ground crumbling

SMELLS
sweet
chemically
bad
good

Popcorn, licorice, peanuts, or fresh vegetables can be the basis for similiar lessons.

When-They-Are-Ready Techniques

A Newspaper

Teachers usually shudder when the cry "Let's do a newspaper!" is uttered. Images of stencils, mimeograph machines, wasted paper, and various committees fussing and fighting race through the mind. One way to overcome these anxieties is to use a bulletin board newspaper that can be changed daily, weekly, or monthly. The teacher and the class can use this newspaper to report current events or specific topics or simply to inspire creative writing.

The title and the various columns of the newspaper can be decided upon by the class. Such topics could include:

Trips	Weather
Interesting Events	Fashion
Class News	Picture of the Week
Personality of the Week	Lost and Found Column
Poetry Corner	Cook's Corner
Riddles	Comics

Upper-grade classes might select an editorial staff to manage the newspaper. Lessons in analyzing daily papers can be integrated into the project to further students' knowledge of journalism. To spark interest in social studies, a fourth-grade teacher used this technique and built the theme of the bulletin board newspaper around Alaska, the current unit of study. A staff was selected to begin *The Alaskan Journal.* Some of the items that appeared on the board included:

WEATHER REPORT

Clear, spring day. Temperature is up to 60°. Wind going north. Expected to warm up even more later in the day.

FASHIONS
THE MINI-SKIRT COMES TO ALASKA!

When the mini-skirts arrived, the people were anxious to see them. But when they saw them, they said that they were too small. When they were told that this is the way they are worn—short—most of the ladies said they were going to sue the person who made them because they would freeze to death if they wore them.

Some said they would not sue. They want to buy some and see what happens.

Some people like them and some don't.

WANT ADS
FOR SALE: A good dog sleigh. Shiny chrome. Sleek and fast. Brand new. Every boy's dream. Call AL 6-2158 after the whale hunt.

SPORTS
IMPORTANT SPORTS MEET
A contest will be held after the whale hunt. The prize will be a camping set. The sections will be on skiing, tobagganing, and other fun-filled sports events. BOYS! Sign up now! The biggest, greatest contest ever held.

Immediately upon the completion of the unit, the class asked if they could continue this type of activity when they moved on to the next unit. This led to the "publication" of *The Hawaiian Aloha News*, which was prepared with as much enthusiasm as *The Alaskan Journal*.

In lower grades children can report news events orally. The teacher can write the news on the chalkboard or on experience charts:

> The elevator stopped running. *Donna*
> My ball fell in the sewer hole. *Tony*
> My mother is going to have a baby. *Kim*

Placing children's names after their comments helps build self-image. In one classroom a child commented, "I know why you put my name after what I said. It was my idea, and you really care about my ideas don't ya'"

Children in lower grades who have the ability to write have been encouraged to become reporters via mimeographed newspaper guidelines developed by one teacher. The form below was reproduced and distributed to a class interested in the life of early man:

CAVE MAN CHATTER

Volume 1, No. 1

Name of Reporter _____

Class _____ Date _____

MAN DISCOVERS FIRE!

Picture of Fire

NEW TOOL DEVELOPED

Lever:

Picture of Lever

News writing develops accuracy and terseness in both form and style. It is one area of written expression that should be encouraged and experimented with throughout all of the grades.

Keeping Diaries

Keeping diaries is another form of writing that can be both practical and creative. An imaginary diary account of a trip to Fairbanks, Alaska, was kept by a fifth-grade class in a New York City classroom in 1958. Several anecdotes from this diary follow:

MONDAY, 11 AUG. 1958

Our boat, the North Star, left yesterday. We were to sail at 9:00 p.m. but they couldn't get it loaded in time. They had to build a cabin on deck for three cows they were taking to an agricultural school en route. It was 11:00 p.m. before we left.

TUESDAY, 12 AUG.

It is pretty rough this morning. They are getting extra ropes to put around the cabin to anchor it so the cows won't go overboard.

SUNDAY, 17 AUG.

Yesterday we stopped at Ketchikan. Miss H. got a ball of crochet cotton, which cost three times as much as we pay at home.

Ketchikan is the salmon-fishing center.

The climate here is mild in winter and cool in summer.

When we reach Juneau we will be in the heart of the Alaskan panhandle.[4]

---

4. *Everyday Writing*. Albany, New York: The University of the State of New York, The State Education Department, Bureau of Elementary Curriculum Development, 1959, pp. 30-31.

Fictitious diary keeping such as this can be used in a study of a neighborhood or community, Latin, Central, or South American countries, industrial areas of the United States, or of any of the continents.

Diaries also afford opportunities for factual reporting. Records can be kept of:

- Daily weather conditions such as temperature and cloud formations.

- Information relating to scientific accomplishments such as an experiment in growing seeds.

- Highlights of class experiences that occur throughout the year.

- Events that occur outside of school life such as family happenings, play activities, personal records of height and weight, or an account of the way time is spent.

Diary writing, besides calling for brevity and accuracy, also provides an outlet for thoughts and emotions. Often class diaries are extended to a child's keeping of a personal diary.

Letter Writing

There are many areas in the curriculum that offer opportunities for meaningful letter writing experiences. Seize these opportunities and encourage children to write. It is not always necessary to have every class member involved in letter writing—sometimes one child may write a letter containing the ideas of all. With children whose vocabulary and skill is limited, teachers may act as a scribe and encourage the children to illustrate their letters.

Several activities can be offered children when they are preparing letters. They can proofread letters for spelling, punctuation, and grammar with another classmate; they can tell what sentence or word they were proudest of in their letters; and they can be encouraged to use one word in their letters that they never used before. The basic rules and forms of letter writing can be discussed with the entire class and reviewed from time to time when needed. When children are acquainted with the many kinds of letters that can be written, they will write them—and they will do it often!

THANK-YOU LETTERS

Thank-you letters can be written to parents who helped the class in some way, the custodian who keeps the school clean, the policeman on the corner, or to a class member who contributed something special. In one school a class celebrated a Thank-You Letter Week during which notes were sent to everyone who did an extra nicety for them. The class complied a list of 33 persons to whom they wrote.

In another school a fifth-grader wrote to the owner of a pet shop thanking him for giving the class a gift of several white mice.

> Dear Sir:
>
> Thank you for the family of mice you gave to our class. I have been very fascinated with their actions and movements. I have studied white mice at home. I have studied the mice and find their reactions to be similar to the ones we have in class.

I have two questions to ask. Would a mouse live
longer if he was in his natural habitat or if he is kept
in a cage as a pet? Again, I thank you for the mice.

PEN PAL LETTERS

Students can have rich experiences corresponding
with pen pals. Pen pals can be from nearby towns or
cities or from a foreign country. In cities where the population is spread out, for example, San Juan or Los Angeles,
children can correspond with intra-city pen pals. This
increases the opportunity for the children meeting one
day and offers an incentive for keeping up an ongoing
letter writing relationship.

GET-WELL LETTERS

Get-well cards, notes, or letters can be sent to classmates, teachers in the school, other school personnel,
community figures, or to convalescent adults. Everyone
appreciates being thought of when absent from school
or work with an illness.

LETTERS OF INVITATION

Letters inviting another class or perhaps a parent in to
see a special classroom display or project can be
composed.

REQUESTS FOR PERMISSION

A letter might be sent to a parent requesting permission to go on a field trip or for permission to bring
in something special from home. A child might also
write for permission to the principal to do something out
of the ordinary, such as beginning a school club or team.

REQUESTS FOR INTERVIEWS

Interviews provide rich experiences for children. Students can write to community figures, school officials, or to parents to request an interview.

LETTERS TO FAMOUS PEOPLE

Letters to famous people such as statesmen, scientists, artists, writers, or sports and entertainment personalities may be written throughout the school year.

On various occasions children have written to United States astronauts at the NASA Manned Spacecraft Center in Houston, Texas. Third-graders sent M. Scott Carpenter a booklet they made called *All About Planets;* fifth-graders dedicated trees on Arbor Day to Virgil I. Grissom and John W. Young and wrote to NASA to tell about it; fourth-graders wrote the following letters to astronauts White and McDivitt.

> Dear Astronauts:
> I wish to congratulate you both for being the first Americans in space for four days. I had read that maybe both of you were going to walk in space. Everybody was excited when you stepped out into space.

> Dear Astronauts White and McDivitt:
> I saw the atmosphere and you in capsule in Cape Kennedy. I hope you have plenty of excitement in the capsule and safely land. I will congratulate you. I wish I can see the future. I saw you on T.V. when you orbited around the earth one or two times in your spaceship. There is no gravity in space so you can float but you need oxygen. You made an accomplishment on the world and earth, I hope you have your daily meal.

Children are always quite excited to receive replies from noted personalities. Letter writing of this nature contains built-in incentives!

FRIENDLY LETTERS

A very successful project in writing friendly letters was initiated in New York when a group of fifth-graders forwarded a batch of letters to soldiers in Viet Nam via New York's *Daily News*.[5] A letter was returned to *The News* from a colonel telling how much the soldiers enjoyed the messages, along with some photographs of men reading them. This kind of an activity, sparked by a creative teacher, was one that had much meaning and interest for his pupils.

Friendly letters can be written to pals, grandmothers, milkmen—or even pets! Children will naturally share many happenings through the writing of a letter to a friend.

NOVELTY LETTERS

Imaginations can run high when a novelty type of letter writing experience is introduced. A third-grader created:

>Dear Columbus:
>You forgot your unbrela.
>>Signed,
>>Mother

Other examples include:

>Dear Pencil:
>>Signed,
>>Paper
>Dear Needle:
>>Signed,
>>Thread

---

5. Phil Santora. "Fifth-Graders Letters Earn An A from G. I.'s." *The Daily News,* September 12, 1966, p. 18.

Dear Pot:
>   Signed,
>   Stove

Novelty letters can also be written after historical facts have been researched: Abraham Lincoln might "write" to Frederick Douglass, Squanto to a Pilgrim, or Harriet Tubman to a slave woman.

REQUESTS FOR INFORMATION

A fifth-grade girl wrote to a government agency to ask:

> Dear Sirs:
>   I have found from three different books that the color of George Washington's hair was red, auburn and dark brown. Most pictures have him with gray hair. Can you tell me what color his hair *really* was?

A reply was sent from Mrs. Mabeth B. Sheppard, who related that:

> The librarian at Mount Vernon tells me that, as a youth, George Washington had dark brown hair, verging on auburn. It started to turn gray during the Revolution and then became completely white.
>   Despite popular misconceptions, George Washington never wore a wig.

Teachers can provide children with the know-how of where to send for information when library materials are unavailable or do not include sufficient data to satisfy the extra-hungry young researcher.

Requesting information from embassies, chambers of commerce, industries, and organizations can also provide letter-writing experiences. Annette Frank Shapiro, on the Bank Street College staff, uses a very novel technique for securing information on the various states. She suggests that children find smaller towns or hamlets listed in an atlas and write to them. Smaller towns rarely receive such requests for information and are very happy to accommodate children from other areas. In a Harlem fifth grade, where this method was employed, children received letters from local mayors, photographs, newspapers, and town-event calendars. Such material made a study of the United States take on new dimensions and provided for an exciting year's work.

LETTERS TO SHARE INFORMATION

Letters can be written to share information about new discoveries or new insights. *The Curious Gerbils,* a booklet published by Elementary Science Study, has this statement on its back cover:

> Let us know other things you do with your gerbils and what you find out about them. If you would like to share your discoveries, thoughts, questions, please write to
> The Gerbils
> Elementary Science Study
> 108 Water Street
> Watertown, Massachusetts 02712

Letters can also be written to congratulate, apologize, or to protest!

Biographical Data Service

Sixth-graders in an Atlanta, Georgia, school originated this service for children in grades four and five. Teachers from the three grades met to plan the details before introducing the idea to the students. The plan was simple. Children in grades four and five were encouraged to write letters to the sixth-grade class asking them for additional information on famous personalities. The letters were brought to the sixth grade and were read aloud by a student; interested children, either alone or in a small group, volunteered to do research on the personality requested; when the work was completed, the child (or children) presented a lesson to the class that requested the information.

Varied presentations were created, including showing a filmstrip, presenting a panel discussion, broadcasting highlights of a person's life over the school's public address system, reading part of a biography on the personality, and presenting art projects in different media. Several children decided to cooperatively plan and write picture biographies for younger classes. These booklets became a part of the classroom library and were used throughout the school year. One group did the necessary research and writing, while others contributed their artistic talents to the production of the booklets.

A total of 50 such biographies, which included personalities from professions, occupations, the literary world, and from the field of sports and entertainment were prepared during the year. This experience was beneficial for the children, for they were able to write in simple terms, and yet receive recognition from teachers, peers, and younger schoolmates.

The Biographical Data Service has been successfully tried in school districts throughout the country. Several teachers have used this device to stir interest in contemporary Negroes. Children have written to Thurgood Marshall, Justice of the Supreme Court, entertainers such as Sidney Poitier and Pearl Bailey, Roy Wilkins, Executive Director of the National Association for the Advancement of Colored People, and newly elected Mayors Carl B. Stokes of Cleveland, Ohio, and Richard G. Hatcher of Gary, Indiana, to obtain information about their lives and their work.

The Service could be correlated into ongoing classroom programs. Children could research past and current mathematicians, scientists, government leaders, statesmen, or other groups of people in the social sciences.

Unusual Happenings

Sometimes an unusual, offbeat experience can be used to motivate children to write. The Chrysanthemum Caper is one technique that can encourage young minds to run wild. One autumn Monday morning, I brought three huge, multi-colored chrysanthemums into a fourth-grade class. The fresh flowers were put into a vase and placed on a table in the room. A lively 15-minute discussion was held about the chrysanthemums. The next day there was additional conversation about the flowers. The children continued to observe them and were asked to record their thoughts about the mums on index cards. This experience continued each day, becoming more and more stimulating. Naturally, toward the end of the week the flowers began to die; the petals fell all over the table and floor, the stems and leaves rotted and curled up, and the water became stagnant. The students in this class observed and creatively wrote humorous and serious stories and poems such as they never had before. Their work was superior.

The Curious Cabbage was another technique used to rouse young interests. It is quite hard for children not to become curious at some point during the school day when a large, green head of cabbage is staring them in the face! The curious cabbage just sat on my desk until near the end of the school day, at which point I pulled a knife from my drawer and dramatically cored the cabbage. As a gift to each child, I presented him with a leaf and told him he could do anything he wanted with it. Some children threw it in the nearest litter container; others, however, played along. Carmen took hers to sleep with her; Rodney studied it for several hours at home and created a poem. The next day we talked and talked about the curious cabbage—how the children felt when they first saw it on my desk, what they thought it was for, and why I gave each one of them a leaf.

The above examples are out of the ordinary, but then again, childhood is filled with extraordinary happenings. Many times the unusual or the unexpected is the very thing that causes wonderment and astonishment, and these are the things that spark new ideas—children's ideas are pure, innocent, and ever so beautiful.

And So They Write

Writing sets a mood and an atmosphere. It helps to develop imagination; it strengthens and adds to vocabulary development. It teaches that stories have plots with people and places running in and out and through them. Writing begins, goes somewhere, and ends! And the words set down on what was once empty paper become a part of time.

Charles writes to tell the world about himself:

YES, I CAN!

I will have the highest Negro office that a Negro ever had.

As I work for my high office I will get a doctoral degree.

I will rule the country well.

I will travel all over the world.

I will make new and better laws.

There shall be bigger and more schools.

Our children shall have bigger playgrounds to play in, and not have to play in the street.

The old buildings will be torn down, and new ones will stand in their places.

I want to be the President of the United States of America.

James tells of his adventure in:

THE MYSTERIOUS TOWER

I was walking along the country road one Halloween night. The clock struck twelve and then I saw an old broken down tower. I went inside because the door was open.

When I got inside the tower, it was dark and gloomy. The door closed. I saw a head with the skin off. It was a skull without a body. Then a ghost came out.

The skull and the ghost were flying in the air. They began playing cards. The ghost played an ace. The skull played a king. Then the skull said, "draw a card." I wasn't petrified at all. In fact, I wasn't even scared. Then the ghost and skull both went away.

I went out the door. I walked into town tricking and treating. When I got home, I fainted.

Diane makes a wish:

ALADDIN'S LAMP

If I could find Aladdin's lamp, I would make a wish
to be a nurse because I like to care for babies. But
since I'm only nine and in the fourth grade, my seed
is still growing. So I guess I'll keep on reading, and
studying until I reach the top.

Ruby Frank and Phillip Kee boast about:

THE NAVAJO

In the proud land of the Navajos
Where mountains and hills stand high
My people find life.
I'm proud to be one of them.
In ages past they have been mislead.
Still, I'm proud to be one of them.
Many of them lack education,
Yet, I'm proud to be one of them.
The population of Navajos is increasing—
The old generation is decreasing,
The new generation is increasing.
Still, I'm proud to be one of them.
I love my country and my people—
Under the clear blue sky
They watch over their flocks and homes
Today, I'm still proud to be one of the
Navajos.[6]

and Donald inquires:

I can't write no story just yet but I wrote this
far so someday I will write a story but not just
yet. does this make me a author anyhow?

6. *Smoke Signals,* February 1968, p. 7. For further information about
this magazine, write to Intermountain School, Post Office Box 345,
Brigham City, Utah 84302, Attention: Wilma L. Victor, Superintendent.

Thus, writing provided an outlet for Charles to express his aspirations; it showed James that he could gain satisfaction by discovering that he can build suspense and cause people to laugh with his clever use of surprise; it paved the way for Diane to imagine and dream; it allowed for individual differences and expressions of pride as in Ruby and Phillip's poem; it gave Donald the right to say he can't, yet express the hope that maybe someday he will!

Writing is many things to many people. In essence, it is a giving up of inner thoughts and feelings by someone to someone. Children do this easily, for they are the ones whose ideas are always fresh and new—even though the same ideas seem old and tired to the adult. Many things they do in life is a first—and so they write about it. Help them along, for if you do, they will not only write, but they will want to write.

For Further Reading

Applegate, Mauree. *Helping Children Write: A Thinking Together About Children's Creative Writing.* Evanston, Illinois: Row, Peterson, 1954.

An excellent text citing many helpful ideas for classroom use on every grade level.

Bauman, Charles. "Sixth Graders Write to England," *Elementary English,* January 1963, pp. 28–9.

The author, a New Jersey educator, tells of a year-long group communication with an equivalent class in a boy's school located in Norfolk, England.

Beck, John M., and Saxe, Richard W., eds. *Teaching the Cultur-ally Disadvantaged Pupil.* Springfield, Illinois: Charles C. Thomas, 1965.

Chapter VI of this text, "Language Arts for the Disadvantaged," authored by Mildred Lennon Wittick of Paterson State College, Wayne, New Jersey, provides good ideas on practical, personal, and creative forms of writing.

Ferebee, June, et al. *They All Want to Write.* New York: Bobbs-Merrill, 1939.
A classic text emphasizing children's potential for unique self-expression.

Hart, Day Leavitt, and Sohn, David A. *Stop, Look, and Write.* New York: Bantam Books, 1964.
This paperback is divided into 20 sections containing over 100 dramatic photographs that can be used to stimulate and motivate many creative writing experiences.

Hopkins, Lee Bennett, and Shapiro, Annette Frank. "The Amazing ABC's," *Today's Catholic Teacher.* October 4, 1968, pp. 11–12.
A list of lively and practical ways to use the ABC's on every grade level.

Taussig, Annette. "How to Kill a Chicken . . . and other Tri-umphs," *Grade Teacher,* March 1968, pp. 140–50.
This article tells how a creative teacher freed children of Mexi-can-American and Negro migrant backgrounds to write spontane-ously and creatively despite their many language barriers.

Winters, Margretta. "Creative Writing: Inside Out," *Elementary English,* January 1963, pp. 88–91.
A grab-bag full of practical ideas that are easy to adapt to any grade level.

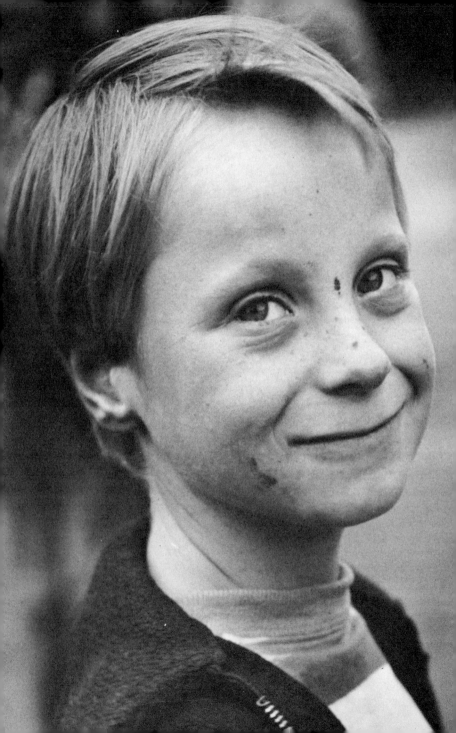

Poetry

"Happiness Falling From The Sky!"

Poetry!

There is nothing better in the field of literature to train ears and flash beautiful word-pictures before young minds. Where else can one find the imagery contained in poems? What other form of writing can say so much in just two or three or ten lines?

Poetry is like many dishes spread out on a smorgasboard table—you go around and select what *you* want! If you want to laugh, there are Ogden Nash, Edward Lear, and Dr. Seuss. If you want to go on adventure, there are many to choose from. If you want a boy-poem or a girl-poem or an Indian poem—you can find it!

Gerald D. McDonald tells us that:

> Poetry can be wittier and funnier than any kind of writing; it can tell us about the world through words we can't forget; it can be tough or it can be tender, it can be fat or lean; it can preach a short sermon or give us a long thought (the shorter the poem, some-

times, the longer the thought). And it does all this through the music of words.[1]

The music of words! Such music should be spread throughout each and every year of a child's life, and it should appear naturally, unforced.

Long before a child enters elementary school, he has heard sounds and rhythms of words. Radio and television advertising, with its jingles and catchy phrases, has filled his ears. Music has made him aware of rhythm, and before he can utter his first words, he will listen to a beat, sway, turn round and round, tap his feet, or clap his hands.

If a child is fortunate, he will have been exposed to nursery rhymes and Mother Goose jingles; he will have had them sung or told to him prior to entering kindergarten. In the busy lives of the families who live in disadvantaged areas, this luxury is sometimes impossible. Time cannot be spent this way—there is too much to do to keep the house running smoothly, to make a living, to provide the basic elements of life. Therefore, it is both the responsibility and the privilege of teachers to introduce Mother Goose rhymes and nonsense jingles to children, for this literature is an introduction to poetry as well as an important part of our literary heritage.

There are many reasons why Mother Goose has lasted through time. The rhymes are filled with action: "Tom, Tom, the piper's son/stole a pig and away he ran." They have characters who become familiar quickly through ludicrous situations such as an old woman

1. Gerald D. McDonald, comp. *A Way of Knowing*. New York: Thomas Y. Crowell, 1959, p. xi.

living in a shoe or a young miss being frightened by a spider. They have repetition of words with alliteration, which young children love to listen to and say: "Hickory, dickory, dock. . . , Little Tommy Tittlemouse . . . , Wee Willie Winkie . . ." They are succinct and they are easily remembered: "Jack be nimble/Jack be quick/ Jack jump over/the candlestick." They pave the road to simple poetry and to beautiful prose: "Here am I/Little Jumping Joan/When nobody's with me/I'm all alone."

Mother Goose is a natural for children, and teachers should make sure they do not miss the lifelong pleasures that only she can give. Soon after Mother Goose, we should introduce poems by those master poets whose work is timeless: Christina Rossetti, Laura Richards, A. A. Milne, Vachel Lindsay, Rachel Field, and Robert Louis Stevenson. Later we should acquaint them with Robert Frost, Carl Sandburg, Langston Hughes, Gwendolyn Brooks, Hilda Conkling, Sara Teasdale, and Eleanor Farjeon.

As in the field of books for children, there is a multitude of poetry volumes. Again the question arises, what poems should we use? The best verse is that which deals with a familiar experience of a child. Naturally the city child does not have the same experiences as the suburban or rural child. The city child's exposure to animals, lakes, meadows, and pastures may be limited. The suburban or rural child may never have been on a train, may never have seen a skyscraper or apartment house, or may not be able to comprehend city noises or the hustle and bustle of city life. Such experiences are provided, however, through various areas of the curriculum and, whenever possible, poetry should naturally relate to ongoing units in social studies, science, music, art, and mathematics. Many children delight in and devour such poems as Carl Sandburg's "Arithmetic"[2] and Eleanor Farjeon's "Geography,"[3] two poems that beautifully depict children's thoughts about these subjects.

With the tremendous variety of poetry available today, it is not difficult to tailor poems to the special needs and individual interests of children. This approach to poetry will contribute much more to the child's appreciation of verse. Too often the unit approach is used, whereby teachers introduce, analyze, and assign poems for memorization for several weeks in the school year and then never offer poetry again. Listening to or producing any type of creative expression cannot be achieved during a rigid and regimented time period. To try to do so will only destroy any love a child has for verse.

The verse you select for use in the classroom should contain vocabulary a child can grasp. It is proper and sometimes necessary to explain one or several words, but to go on and on with a vocabulary lesson will detract from the poem you want to introduce. Similarly the meaning of the poem should require little explanation. "Some poems cannot be explained," states Herbert Read. "They shimmer in the mind suggestively, like tantalizing puzzles."[4] The taste for poetry is soured by the dissection of words, phrases, and lines:

2. *Ibid.*
3. Eleanor Farjeon. *Eleanor Farjeon's Poems for Childhood.* Philadelphia: Lippincott, 1951.
4. Herbert Read. *This Way Delight.* New York: Pantheon, 1956, p. 140.

What does this word mean?
What does this phrase refer to?
What does the author really mean?

If a lengthy discussion about a poem is necessary, the selection is either not right for the class or the moment. Poems should be shared for their rhythm, their visual imagery, and for the emotional response a child feels when he hears or reads them. Poems should be presented simply. Many times a short statement such as: "I am going to read you a poem about an elephant!" or "Hey! Sharon brought us a poem about a moving van, today!" is sufficient motivation.

The follow-up to a poem is also an important part of poetry programs. We should not ask children if they like the verse just read. If children have the desire to say something, they will say it. If they do not, let the poem end with its own final words.

Poetry programs throughout the grades should have a variety of rhymed and free verse. Beginning in the second and third grades, free verse can be introduced. The haiku form is a perfect introduction to free verse, and it can be read and used prior to going on to poems written by contemporary poets. Langston Hughes' "April Rain Song,"[5] Carl Sandburg's "Fog,"[6] and Lilian Moore's "Rain River"[7] are examples of fine free verse to use with young children.

In the upper grades narrative verse and ballads should be gradually introduced along with poetry that evokes

5. Langston Hughes. *The Dream Keeper*. New York: Alfred A. Knopf, 1932.
6. Carl Sandburg. *Early Moon*. New York: Harcourt Brace, 1930.
7. Lilian Moore. *I Feel the Same Way*. New York: Atheneum, 1967.

emotions, stirs the imagination, and causes children to think like they never have before. A perfect example of such poetry is *The Ballad of the Burglar of Babylon,* by Elizabeth Bishop (Farrar, 1968). This poem tells of Micuçú, a fugitive who flees to the hill of Babylon in Rio de Janeiro. The extraordinary woodcuts by Ann Grifalconi highlight this stirring, action-packed story.

The Index to Children's Poetry (H. W. Wilson, 1942; *Supplements,* 1954, 1965), compiled by John and Sara Brewton, is an excellent resource for the classroom teacher. These reference volumes, which can be found in most children's libraries, give the title, subject, author, and first lines of poems that can be found in well known collections.

Teachers should take the time to read poetry to their classes everyday. Children should *hear* poems, for poetry is created to be heard. If we read poetry regularly, it will not be unusual to hear children ask to have their favorite verses read over and over again.

Enriching Children's Experiences with Poetry

An appreciation for poetry can sometimes be developed by encouraging children to look for poems in books, magazines, and newspapers. Children can aid in producing poetry anthologies or poetry files for classroom libraries. These collections can be bound into booklets, filed in shoeboxes within the classroom, or be put into large, brown manila envelopes and tacked under the chalkboard. Poems can be grouped and organized by a class committee. Specific headings might include: Months of the Year, Funny Poems, Seasonal

Poems, Science Poems, or Poems of Mystery. Poem cycles can be developed on topics such as Streets, Brothers and Sisters, Animals, or Houses.

Children who contribute poems to a class collection can record their names on them. Opportunities will frequently arise when such files will be useful. For instance, when a child is disruptive or in an unhappy frame of mind, the teacher might save the day by reading *the* poem that he or she contributed to the class—perhaps just for a boost of morale. One teacher in a Harlem classroom uses an old adage in verse form as a means of discipline. If a child is unwieldly, she merely comments in a dramatic tone:

> Let no one say, and say it to your shame,
> That all was quiet here—until you came!

Another appropriate time to use the file might be when the first snow of the year begins to fall from the sky. Poems under Snow or Winter might be shared. Selections might include "Snowstorm" by Hilda Conkling,[8] a poem that compares snowflakes to daisies, "Dragon Smoke" by Lilian Moore,[9] a free-verse poem telling about how one's breath looks on a cold, cold day, or David McCord's "The Frost Pane,"[10] a humorous account of breathing on a windowpane in summer and in winter. An original poem might also be read—perhaps one written by a class member, someone from a former class, or one by a child from another place.

8. Hilda Conkling. *Poems by a Little Girl.* New York: Frederick A. Stokes, 1920.
9. Lilian Moore, *op. cit.*
10. David McCord. *Every Time I Climb a Tree.* Boston: Little Brown, 1967.

There will be times when the interest in shared poetry will be so high that further activities might be planned. For example, children can effectively pantomine or dramatize poetry. One third-grade classroom in Virginia recently produced a Mother Goose Festival. The children represented such characters as Jack Sprat and his wife, Wee Willie Winkie, and Wynken, Blynken, and Nod. They acted out the familiar situations in an assembly program for the kindergarten, and first and second grades. Simple props and scenery was constructed, costumes were made, and background music was found and used to enhance the production.

Another teacher in Cleveland planned a similar program entitled Nature and the Universe. Children became stars, planets, and comets, and they dramatized and recited original verse and poems they had collected throughout the school year.

Children on every grade level enjoy relating poetry to art experiences, and various art media can be employed to interpret poetry. Moods, feelings, scenes, or characters can be painted, drawn, or sculptured. Attractive displays can be made by featuring a child's artwork along with selected poems. Using realia can sometimes provide further motivation for children to enjoy a poem. For example, peels from lemons and apples can be placed on a table to entice children to read Aileen Fisher's "Skins"[11]; bursted balloons can be tacked on a bulletin board along with Patricia Hubbell's unique "Balloons"[12]:

11. Aileen Fisher. *Runny Days, Sunny Days.* New York: Abelard-Schuman, 1933.
12. Patricia Hubbell. *Catch Me a Wind.* New York: Atheneum, 1968, p. 4.

BALLOONS

Pop!

     POP!

          POp!

  pop

        ying

   loon   l

  l   s were f

 a

 B

What can we do with them? What can we do with
                                 them?
What can we do with the dead balloons?
Nothing! Nothing!
No thing can we do with them.
Only remember them, think and remember them.
That is the way of the bright balloons.

Designing greeting cards can be another incentive to
share poems. Children can select an appropriate poem
and illustrate it. The cards can be used for classmates',
parents', or friends' birthdays, as get-well messages, or
they can be sent on special holidays. Many of the suggestions offered in the previous chapter can also be
utilized to enrich children's experiences with poetry.

Poems By and About Negroes

While visiting a high school with an 85 percent Negro
enrollment in Newark, New Jersey, I asked a senior
honors class to raise their hands *only* if they knew all
three poets that were to be mentioned—Henry Wads-
worth Longfellow, Carl Sandburg, Robert Frost. The

response was 100 percent. The question was then posed: "How many had ever heard of all three of the following poets—Paul Laurence Dunbar, Gwendolyn Brooks, and Langston Hughes?" Five hands were raised!

This experience was not surprising, for when this same question is posed to adults, the response is usually similar. It is very unfortunate that poetry by Negro authors has not received the attention it warrants. Very successful attempts have been made to raise the self-image of the black child by introducing Negro poets to children. There are many excellent anthologies containing their work (see Appendix III: Outstanding Volumes of Negro Poetry). Humor, pathos, and highly imaginative verse for young children appears in *Bronzeville Boys and Girls* (Harper, 1956) by Gwendolyn Brooks, the first Negro to win the Pulitzer Prize for Poetry in 1950. Older children will appreciate and enjoy the works of Langston Hughes, Paul Laurence Dunbar, Joseph Seamon Cotter, Jr., Countee Cullen, and Phillis Wheatley. The work of these great poets can serve as a means of showing that verse has universal appeal—that all mankind can relate to the message poetry conveys. Acquainting children with Negro poets also gives recognition to the outstanding achievements the Negro has made to the field of literature.

Teachers should utilize poetry by and about Negroes and integrate it into classroom learnings. Children, whether they are from the Cumberlands or Bronzeville, U.S.A., will develop an understanding and feeling for black people through their writings.

Writing Poetry

If poems are read frequently to children and if they are exposed to and made aware of beautiful language, they will naturally acquire an ability to express themselves in verse. Children should be acquainted with many diverse forms of poetry. When poetry is mentioned a child almost immediately thinks of rhymed verse: "One, two, buckle my shoe . . ." "Hey diddle, diddle . . ." "Me-you-two-blue . . ."

In writing poetry, rhyme is not the essence. Children in disadvantaged areas often have more problems writing rhyme than they do free verse. This is not to say this area of writing should be totally avoided. Some children find it comfortable to produce couplets, triplets, and/or quatrains. They enjoy listening to the sing-song of word phrases and delight in writing it. One third-grader created "Prize Fight" while viewing a professional boxing match on television:

PRIZE FIGHT
Give him a left and give him a right.
Don't you dare let him win the fight.
Go into him and then come out
Watch that right! Knock him out!

A fourth-grader wrote:

MY SEED
The seed is growing deep inside
It can not hide, It can not hide.
It shoves and pushes it bangs and kicks
And one day the world will know me.

The limerick form is a favorite among older boys and

girls. The humorous passages of Edward Lear can set an example of style and form. The limerick is written in five lines: the first, second, and fifth lines rhyme, the third and fourth lines have a different rhyme scheme. Examples of Lear's limericks can be found in May Hill Arbuthnot's popular anthology *Time for Poetry* (Scott-Foresman, 1951).

Writing poetry can grow out of a lesson and/or discussion on the five senses or the use of similes. Discussions might be held on a one-to-one basis when a teacher feels that a child or a group of children is ready for enrichment.

Introducing unrhymed verse forms such as haiku, senryu, cinquain, and sijo has become very popular in middle-grade classes—particularly those in disadvantaged areas—for they produce rewarding results. There are many reasons for their appeal. The forms are easy to construct; rhyming, meter, and balance are not needed; they can be written about any subject; and they provide the encouragement and satisfaction of completing an assignment—something that is important for all children.

In introducing the various forms to children, it is interesting to arouse their curiosity before describing the formula. For example, I ask children to tell me what they think *haiku,* means. I ask: "Would you *eat* it? *Sleep* on it? *Save* it? What *would* you do with it?" Then I ask: "What country do you think the word might come from?" and I list the various responses on the chalkboard. Cinquain is usually guessed as coming from France or Spain since *cinq* is French for five and *cinco* is five in Spanish. Children are quite surprised to learn that the term was coined by an American woman born in Brooklyn Heights, New York—Adelaide Crapsey.

I also try to have the children discover the form by reading several examples. Next, I place an example on the chalkboard, reinforce their discoveries, and let those who wish create some of their own. When they have completed their work, I have them volunteer to read the finished product to the class. Finally, a display is planned to show off their compositions.

Children naturally take to these forms and use them throughout the year in various classroom projects.

Haiku

The haiku is an ancient form of Japanese poetry. It is written in three lines with a five-seven-five syllable count respectively. The purpose of the haiku is to present a single thought or observation particularly related to nature and indicating a season of the year. Excellent examples of haiku poetry that serve as a good introduction to the correct form appear in several inexpensive volumes listed at the end of this chapter.

Emily Stegossi from the Stephen Girard School, Philadelphia, discusses the seasons of the year prior to introducing a haiku lesson. She lists the four seasons in one column, three senses in another, and asks the children to offer images:

	SIGHT	HEARING	SMELL
SPRING	blue skies	birds	honeysuckle
	robins	insects	roses
SUMMER	butterflies	crickets	summer rains
	green grass	brooks	salty, sea air

	SIGHT	HEARING	SMELL
FALL	colored leaves pumpkins	crackling leaves	burning leaves apple cider
WINTER	snow icicles	sleigh bells winds	pine trees roasted chestnuts

The following haiku were created by her sixth-grade students:

> The rain is a bore.
> It tries to spoil the fine day.
> I think it's jealous!

• • •

> Wild game wing their way
> Following their head leader
> Through the horizon.

Senryu

Senryu was named for the Japanese poet who originated this verse form. Senryu is the same form as the haiku, but it differs in that the topic may deal with anything—it is not restricted to references to nature or seasons. The senryu form concentrates on a single idea or the image of a moment. The use of this form gives a child the opportunity to express his ideas on any subject.

> The wham of the bat!
> The yelling of the large crowd!
> "Out!" calls the empire.
>
> *Fourth-grader*

> Go home little girl—
> Your parents are calling you.
> Go home! And don't cry.
>
> *Fifth-grader*

Cinquain

> Endless
> Dirt road, real long,
> Always lonely, quiet—
> Feeling of no one loving you;
> Lonely.

This cinquain was sent to me by Sister M. Jeremy, S.S.M., of Wildwood, Pennsylvania, who stated;

> I had the children write a cinquain. It is amazing how such a short piece can hold such thought and beauty. I like especially "Endless." (This child) wrote hers just when her older sister was getting married and moving to Texas. She expressed her loneliness extremely well. . . .

One of the reasons children respond to cinquains is that the sensitivity and delicateness of the form almost commands an immediate reaction. Cinquain was originated by Adelaide Crapsey (1878-1914). It was not until a year before her death that she wrote and perfected the cinquain. The form contains five lines, generally in iambic cadence, and has a two-four-six-eight-two syllable count respectively. A second form of cinquain devised by a classroom teacher as a form of word play is:

Line 1—One word to give a title

Line 2—Two words to describe the title

Line 3—Three words to express action concerning the title

Line 4—Four words to express feeling about the title

Line 5—One word, which is another word for the title.

Children enjoy this form of cinquain also. The fourth-grade class of Frances Weismann in East Paterson, New Jersey, experimented with it and created such verses as these:

Eyes
Ever watching
Fiery, gentle, awake
Tears, expressing thoughts openly
Windows

• • •

Darkness
Black screen
Silent, still, invisible
Lonely, gloomy, hidden joy
Night.

Sijo

Sijo is a verse form that dates back to fourteenth century Korea. In English the sijo form is written in six lines, each line containing six to eight syllables. Sijo is more difficult for children than the previous forms and should not be introduced until a child can handle syllablication easily. There are two excellent texts containing examples of sijo translated from the original by Peter H. Lee (see For Further Reading at the end of this chapter).

Children find this verse form lovely to listen to and read. If preceded by lessons with the haiku and cinquain form, sijo can prove to be a challenging writing experience. Recently an experiment with a fifth-grade class in Harlem produced the following results:

BALLERINAS

Lovely ballerinas dancing
On their toes. They twirl round and round
Gracefully! Their heads in the air—
Lovely maidens floating on air—
Jump up swiftly and calmly
And twirl around all the night long

SNOW FLAKES

Hooray for white things falling
Fluffy white flakes of joy
Happiness falling from the sky
The feeling makes you shake.
A white wonderland comes in view
Hooray! Hooray! for snow.

Audio-Visual Aids

Recordings, filmstrips, and films of poetry should be used at appropriate times for they can play a vital part in the sharing of and appreciation for verse.

Folkways/Scholastic Records Book Combinations, 906 Sylvan Avenue, Englewood Cliffs, New Jersey 07632, offers the young child *Hi Diddle Diddle,* a 7 inch LP and paperback book with a series of musical nursery rhymes, and *Rocket in My Pocket/Teeny Tiny Woman,* 7 inch LP and two paperbacks featuring nursery rhymes, riddles, and tongue twisters. For older children, offerings include *An Anthology of Negro Poetry for Young People,* compiled and read by Arna Bontemps, and *The Dream Keeper,* read by Langston Hughes. For a complete listing of the material available, write for the company's catalog.

Weston Woods, Weston, Connecticut 06880, offers a two-record set entitled *Poetry Parade* that can be used with children of various ages. The poets David McCord, Harry Behn, Aileen Fisher, and Karl Kushin read their work and talk about what they have written or how they felt when they wrote specific pieces. Poems about animals, insects, weather and the seasons, and children's adventures are included in this series.

Full-color films and filmstrips have been produced by Weston Woods also. Nursery rhymes, work by Edward Lear and Ogden Nash, Japanese haiku, and Ernest Laurence Thayer's classic poem "Casey at the Bat" are featured to create moods and the pictures the poet has drawn by words.

Caedmon Records, Inc., 505 Eighth Avenue, New York, New York 10018, produced a four-volume set of 12 inch LPs entitled *A Gathering of Great Poetry for Children*. First-rate poets and poems have been brought together by Richard Lewis, for use with children in grades kindergarten through sixth. Julie Harris, Cyril Ritchard, and David Wayne read poems, and Carl Sandburg, Robert Frost, Dylan Thomas, and T. S. Eliot read their own work.

Caedmon also produces recordings of Mother Goose, read by Cyril Ritchard, Celeste Holm, and Boris Karloff. A reading entitled *Madeline and Other Bemelmans* is done by Carol Channing.

Spoken Arts, Inc., 59 Locust Avenue, New Rochelle, New York 10801, makes available such recordings as *You Read to Me, I'll Read to You*, read by John Ciardi. Various works of Mother Goose, Lewis Carroll, and Robert Louis Stevenson are also produced.

Enrichment Teaching Materials, 246 Fifth Avenue, New York, New York 10001, manufacturers *Prose and*

Poetry Enrichment Records, a six-volume set suitable for upper elementary and junior and senior high school grades. Selections include Longfellow's "Hiawatha" and "Paul Revere's Ride," Browning's "The Pied Piper of Hamelin," and Kipling's "If" and "Annabel Lee." The records are narrated by E. G. Marshall, Edward Mulhare, Dane Clark, Bennett Cerf, Arnold Moss, and Clifton Fadiman.

Most of this material can be purchased with National Defense Education Act (NDEA) and/or Elementary and Secondary Education Act (ESEA) funds.

Audio-visual aids can play an exciting role in poetry programs. High quality material is being produced to combine the finest of children's literature with flawless performance and perfect enunciation. Children will enjoy listening to the spoken word and viewing the beautiful imagery only poetry can convey.

For Further Reading

READINGS ON SHORT VERSE FORMS

Henderson, Harold. *Haiku in English.* Rutland, Vermont: Charles E. Tuttle, 1967.

This paperback, available for $1.00, includes an excellent chapter, "Writing and Teaching Haiku," which will be of great value to the elementary school teacher.

Hopkins, Lee Bennett. "Breaking the Verse Barrier," *Catholic School Journal,* October 1967 pp. 52–3.

Haiku, cinquain, and sijo are discussed; samples of children's writing are included.

—————. "For Creative Fun, Let Them Try a Cinquain," *Grade Teacher,* December 1966, pp. 83, 108.

Two forms of the cinquain verse form are presented; samples

of children's work from Fair Lawn, New Jersey, and Harlem, New York, are included.

————. "From Trudeau's Garden." *Elementary English,* October 1967, pp. 613–14.

A detailed biographical account on the life of Adelaide Crapsey, the originator of the cinquain verse form. Work from the author's book *Verse* is cited, along with examples of children's work in urban and suburban areas. A poem entitled "Adelaide Crapsey," by Carl Sandburg is also included.

> (NOTE: The above articles by Lee Bennett Hopkins can be purchased in a brochure entitled *Breaking the Verse Barrier,* for 25¢. It is available from Bank Street College Book Store, 69 Bank Street, New York, New York 10014.)

Lee, Peter H., translator. *Anthology of Korean Poetry.* New York: John Day, 1964.

————. *Korean Literature: Topics and Themes.* Tucson, Arizona: Association for Asian Studies, University of Arizona Press, 1965.

Examples of sijo can be found in this text.

READINGS ON POETRY

Arnstein, Flora J. *Poetry in the Elementary Classroom.* New York: Appleton-Century-Crofts, 1962.

How do you interest children in poetry? How do you get them to write it? What can a teacher do on being required to teach poetry when he feels his background in the subject is inadequate? These questions are expertly answered in this publication of the National Council of Teachers of English.

Cullum, Albert. *Push Back the Desks.* New York: Citation Press, 1967.

This volume is filled with creative experiences; however, the chapter "Poetry Pot" will give you specific ideas on using poetry with children throughout the grades.

Diffin, Leslye T. "Opening the Door to Poetry," *The Instructor,* October 1966, pp. 34–+.

Poetry as used creatively in the primary and early middle grades is presented.

Hopkins, Lee Bennett. "Negro Poets: Through the Music of Their Words," *Elementary English,* February 1968, pp. 206–8.
Brief biographies and samples of the work of Langston Hughes, Paul Laurence Dunbar, and Gwendolyn Brooks are presented.

Wickens, Elaine. "Please Don't Tell the Children," *Young Children,* October 1967, pp. 15–8.
The author discusses the creativity developed by looking at and listening to a child's response to a poem.

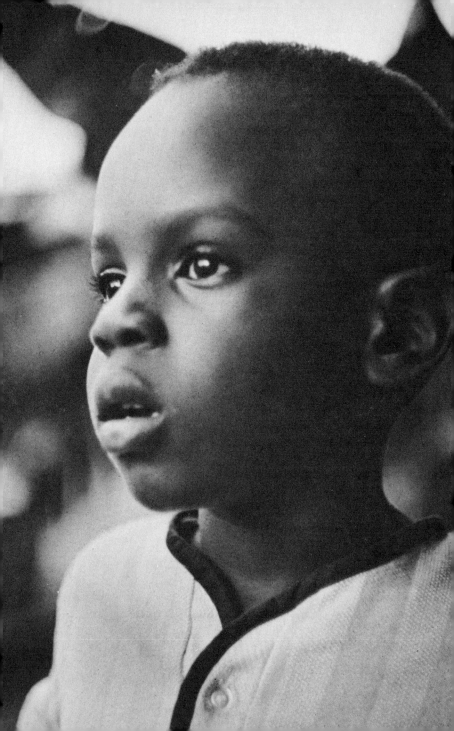

Oral Language Activities
The Spoken Word

A DAY BEGINS in the life of a child:

> "Good morning, Ma."
> "Good morning, son. Sleep well?"
> "Yeah. What's for breakfast?"
> "Whatcha' want?"
> "Anything. Cereal and milk!"

A day continues:

> "Wanna' play stickball with me?"
> "Yeah!"
> "Let's go to the schoolyard and play."
> "Great! Let's go!"

A day ends:

> "Shouldn't you be in bed by now? Shut off the TV and get to bed."
> "O.K. Good night Dad."
> "Good night, son."

The spoken word! It is used everyday in a variety of situations. It is the basic tool of communication—the primary form of verbal language. The child learns to use speech early in infancy. He begins by babbling, gradually making intelligible sounds—then he utters a word, a phrase, a sentence. He can communicate!

Speech patterns used to communicate in the home usually present few problems for the young child; he imitates and learns the patterns employed in his immediate environment—the patterns familiar to both family and peers. It is when the child goes outside his immediate environment that he may find himself frustrated and unable to communicate with others. If he is among the vast majority who are fluent in English, he has little trouble adjusting to new situations that occur within the context of his social milieu. He can ask about things, tell of his anxieties, and communicate feelings, thoughts, and attitudes.

Children who come from poorly-languaged homes or from homes where English is not spoken at all often cannot cope with communication in a strange environment. They remain silent or speak in short, broken phrases. They do not speak up in classrooms; they seem to be unaware of what is going on. They are lost. The rural child, the urban disadvantaged, the Southern Negro, the child with nonstandard speech patterns, the Indian child, and the child who recently arrived from Puerto Rico are all burdened with and torn between their mother tongue and the speech patterns used in the greater world.

Improving the oral communication of these children is

a long and difficult task. They hear one type of oral language in the classroom spoken by the teacher, they hear another from their peers, and they hear still another in their home environs. The school day is short, and there are many areas to cover. The school must be prepared, however, to develop ways to meet the speech needs of students. One of the primary aims of the school should be to aid the child to develop his full capacity as an individual. Today's complex world demands citizens who are highly verbal and able to communicate in acceptable language patterns. Therefore, the school must provide activities that will make proper use of the English language an integral part of the child's learning experience. Through this process the school will produce a child who can function in the great variety of roles needed for successful living today.

Children should be taught that just as there are different behavioral patterns, there are different language patterns and styles for different social situations. As professional adults we can cite a countless number of language roles used in our own lives—we speak one way as a teacher in the classroom, another with teachers in the faculty room, and still another at professional meetings. At home we change our language style and adapt it to family living; we change it again at the baseball game, at a coffee klatch with neighbors, at the opening of a new art gallery, or at a Saturday night cocktail party.

Children should be made aware of these differences. They should not be ashamed of the language used in play with peers or especially of the language used in their homes. They should not be made to feel that there is only one way to speak, for if they do, their frustrations will mount, making them totally confused and thwarted.

The school day provides opportunities for many exciting oral language activities. Children should be allowed to tell something each day, if they so choose. They should be encouraged to share their experiences orally.

In a third-grade classroom recently a child came to school bubbling with some information he wanted to share with his teacher. The first five minutes she was busy discussing something with another faculty member. Then the bell rang. The child was told to sit down and get ready for opening exercises. The flag was saluted, a patriotic song was sung, and then the class was instructed to: "Take out your arithmetic books."

The child was very uneasy, obviously disturbed. He wanted so badly to talk about something. A chance to speak did not come that morning. The rest of his school day was a waste for him. After school there was no one home—no one to listen to his story about a dead cat he had seen in the gutter outside his apartment house, something that greatly bothered him. If this child had the opportunity to tell his classroom teacher about this experience, perhaps the learnings that occurred that day would have been more beneficial.

I always suggest that a few minutes each and every day be spent allowing children to freely converse with one another or to participate in a planned discussion with the entire class. Here views can be exchanged, ideas can be clarified, and an understanding of the amenities of discussion can be developed. Such an activity should not be considered a frill or a waste of time. We all know what it is like to want to share something. How many times do we rush to the telephone to tell our friends of exciting happenings in life:

> I just discovered Phillip's first tooth!
> Nat got the promotion!
> We became grandparents today!

We cannot contain the excitement. We have to share—communicate—let others know that something has happened to us!

Children have more to share than we do, for they are always learning. We take for granted the surprise we felt when we first saw something new. The awe is no longer there when the curtain rises in the theatre, when we smell a bunch of fresh carnations, or when we look at the marvels of nature. As adults we should keep in mind the wonder of childhood—the magic, the mystery, and the miraculous.

A few minutes devoted to a free flow of conversation will add greatly to the rest of the day, to the hours spent on teaching the basics, to the years of learning about life and its many complex components. Small talk can be big talk, and it is an integral part of the curriculum and of life itself.

Use of the Tape Recorder

Roberto, a fourth-grader, was sitting next to the teacher's desk anxiously waiting for her to turn on the dial of the tape recorder.

"Listen!" said Mrs. Allocca. "We are going to hear Roberto read a poem he read at the beginning of the year, and then hear the way he read it yesterday."

The recorder was turned on. Roberto and the rest of the class listened attentively. After a few seconds, Roberto remarked: "Is that me? Man, I don't believe it. Are you puttin' me on?"

Minutes later the class heard the same Roberto reading the same poem. The class was amazed at the speaking skills acquired in five and a half school months, but they were not half as astonished as the beaming Roberto, a new arrival from Santa Clara, Cuba.

The tape recorder is an all-important tool in developing oral language experiences in elementary classrooms. They are widely available today, and their operation is simple enough for even young children to manipulate themselves. The anecdote above shows one way in which a recorder can bring an early awareness to how speaking skills can be improved. Creative expression in other areas of language arts can also be enhanced if children are encouraged and allowed to use a tape recorder. Original stories, poems, and songs can be put on tape and played back for the class to hear.

In one of my sixth-grade classes, the children often selected favorite poems to read and record on tape. One day Richard, a quiet, sullen child who rarely participated in such activities, brought in an African war song he had found in a book of poetry. He showed me the poem and requested me to read it to the class. I stopped everything! As soon as the children were ready, I read the poem.

"Read it again," Richard shouted when I finished. I read it again. This time, however, he began to beat upon his desk with a ruler, a beat that perfectly matched the cadence of the poem.

"Let's tape it," he exclaimed! "You read it Mr. Hopkins, and I'll beat it out. I want to do that instead of reading a poem, O.K.?" (Little did I know that at that very moment I created a Frankenstein. By the end of the year I had read approximately 20 poems to the beat, beat, beat of Richard's enthusiastic drumming.)

Richard's idea led to many new, exciting experiences. We began to discuss how effective the drumming sounds were as a background for poetry. Soon other children were looking for sound effects and recordings to suit the moods of their poetry selections. Within a month we had enough material to plan and produce a Poetry and Music Festival.

Intraschool broadcasts, taped in advance, are usually more effective than those presented live. In most schools, built-in facilities provide for broadcasting from a public address system. Programs taped in advance can be enriched with sound effects and musical backgrounds. An interesting series of broadcasts entitled "This Was the Day" was presented by fourth-graders in Newark, New Jersey. Historical events, birthdates of famous people, holidays, and current local, national, and international happenings were carefully researched. A script was written, put on tape, and broadcast to other classes during a time convenient to their teachers.

On the morning of April 5, 1968—the day after the tragic assassination of Dr. Martin Luther King, Jr.—one of the children brought in a recording of Dr. King's famous speech delivered during the March on Washington, August 28, 1963. The class discussed the death of this Nobel Peace Prize winner, collected data about his life from reference books and from the morning newspapers, and produced a moving broadcast entitled "This Was the Day that the World Became Sad." The upper grades in the school listened intently to one of the most moving speeches in history— ". . . I have a dream . . . I have a dream . . ." Following each of these broadcasts, the tapes were lent to classes that wanted to follow up with additional activities.

In another school a sixth-grade class effectively produced a tape of *Madame Butterfly*, to tie in with an ongoing social studies unit on Japan. The children found a version of the opera written on a child's level, created a script from it, and recorded their efforts. For background effects, they played several of the work's famous arias, dramatically highlighting the production.

Foreign language programs in the elementary school are becoming increasingly important today. Enrichment programs and methodology related to teaching English as a second language offers numerous uses for the tape recorder. Many elementary schools that teach foreign languages have set up foreign tape exchanges with children in other lands, thus replacing pen pal programs. Hearing children's voices from other countries or from other parts of the United States can be quite exciting to all the children involved in such a program.

For foreign-born youngsters, or those with nonstandard speech patterns, tapes can be used for drill exercises. The teacher, or a student, can dictate simple sentences such as: "I have four brothers. How many do you have?" The child can repeat the same phrase, play it back, and listen, checking to hear if he pronounced each word correctly.

Tape recorders can make possible many stimulating projects and can enrich oral language activities in all classrooms.

Choral Speaking

Choral speaking is an activity that can contribute to the appreciation and enjoyment of poetry as well as provide a worthwhile learning experience on any grade level and with any group of children.

The easiest form of choral speaking is the REFRAIN TYPE. Here children merely repeat the refrain or a frequently repeated line of a longer poem. After hearing a selection several times, children quickly learn when the line will appear and reappear, and they will wait anxiously for their cue to participate.

A second type of arrangement is TWO-PART SPEAKING. Two groups of children take a part of the poem. A good example of the two-part form is the nursery rhyme:

RIDING

This is the way the ladies ride:	GIRLS
Tri, tre, tre, tree: tri, tre, tre, tree!	ALL
This is the way the ladies ride:	GIRLS
Tri, tre, tre, tree; tri, tre, tre, tree!	ALL

This is the way the gentlemen ride:	BOYS
Gallop-a-trot, gallop-a-trot!	ALL
This is the way the gentlemen ride:	BOYS
Gallop-a-trot, gallop-a-trot!	ALL
This is the way the farmers ride:	BOYS
Hobbledy-hoy, hobbledy-hoy!	GIRLS
This is the way the farmers ride:	BOYS
Hobbledy-hoy, hobbledy-hoy!	GIRLS

LINE-A-CHILD arrangements are somewhat difficult, yet they give each child a chance to speak one or more lines alone. The difficulty arises from the necessity for precision of delivery.

In PART-SPEAKING varied groups of children take parts of the selection. The teacher has the responsibility of knowing which child can handle the various speaking assignments. Here is one example of part-speaking:

IF YOU'RE GOOD
Author Unknown

Santa Claus will come tonight	BOYS
If you're good	ALL
And do what you know is right,	GIRLS
As you should,	ALL
Down the chimney he will creep,	SOLO
Bringing you a woolly sheep	SOLO
And a doll that goes to sleep	SOLO
If you're good.	ALL
Santa Claus will drive his sleigh	BOYS
Through the wood,	ALL
But he'll come around this way,	GIRLS
If you're good	ALL
With a wind-up bird that sings,	SOLO
And a puzzle made of rings,	SOLO

Jumping jacks, and funny things,
    If you're good.   ALL

He will bring you cars that go   BOYS
    If you're good   ALL
And a rocking-horsey, oh,   GIRLS
    If only he would!   SOLO
And a dolly that can sneeze,   SOLO
    That says—Mama!—when you squeeze,
He'll bring you some of these   SOLO
    If you're good.   ALL

Santa grieves when you are bad,   BOYS
    As he should;   ALL
But it makes him very glad   SOLO
    When you're good;
He is wise and he's a dear,   SOLO
    Just do right and never fear   SOLO
He'll remember you each year—   ALL
    If you're good!

The most difficult type of choral speech is UNISON-SPEAKING, for it involves all the children speaking at the same time. Perfect timing, balance, phrasing, inflection, and pronunciation are required. This takes much practice and is quite time-consuming. Usually the time spent on unison-speaking is not worth the effort when working with poorly-languaged children.

Programs of choral speaking can be planned and enhanced with lighting effects and with interesting staging techniques, such as having children stand in a semi-circle, scattering them around the stage, or interspersing simple dance and mime with their readings.

The selection of material available in this area is vast. A teacher can find poems that are suitable for his class in many anthologies of verse. He can also find books of choral speaking in which arrangements have already been worked out. Rosalind Hughes has collected two such anthologies;[1] Charlotte Lee has prepared dramatic arrangements of Langston Hughes' "The Negro Speaks of Rivers," John Vance Cheney's "The Kitchen Clock," and Walter de le Mare's "The Cupboard," in an excellent discussion entitled "Choric Interpretation."[2]

Choral speaking helps develop good speech, provides the timid child with a degree of self-confidence, and gives many pleasurable moments of enrichment to language arts classes.

Creative Dramatics

Thinking, daydreaming, imagining, playing, doing, and acting are all components of the art of being somewhere, something, or someone else. In the earliest years children's play is filled with acting. The block corner in the nursery and kindergarten is the place where young boys instantly become grown-up men—putting out fires, constructing bridges, or being at war with an enemy. A doll corner is "I am the Mommy. I'll take care of you, baby. I'll do the dishes and wash the floors and change your diapers and watch TV—just like *my* Mommy!"

1. Rosalind Hughes. *Let's Enjoy Poetry: An Anthology of Children's Verse for Kindergarten, Grades I, II, and III with Suggestions for Teaching*. Boston: Houghton-Mifflin, 1958. (*Grades IV, V, and VI* was published in 1961.)
2. Charlotte Lee. "Choric Interpretation," in Mabel Wright Henry, ed. *Creative Experiences in Oral Language*. Champaign, Illinois: National Council of Teachers of English, 1967, pp. 13-30.

When children participate in dramatic play, they cooperate with one another, they begin to feel the need for exchanging ideas, they speak, they listen, their vocabularies improve, readiness for reading takes place, and pathways are opened to the direct teaching phases of written communication.

Dramatic play is a natural step to creative dramatics. Stories in books become magic wands that can transform children with a flash of the hand into Cinderellas, ogres and ogresses, knights, and cops and robbers. Informal story dramatizations can be effectively used in both lower- and middle-grade classrooms. Plays can be produced by playing and acting out spontaneous dialogue and action. Questions can be posed to children such as: What scene shall we begin with? Where does the play take place? Who are the characters in the story? What are they like? How will they walk, talk, move, grimace, and react to the various situations presented in the story?

Poems, books, and films can all lead to the development of story dramatizations. An innovative program executed by a second-grade class of average children in New Jersey was developed through a multi-media approach. The children in Mrs. Pearl Rabin's class were studying communities around the world, emphasizing children of other lands. Where possible, the teacher brought in a story indigenous to the country being studied. As a culminating activity, the children planned an assembly program. Through the use of experience chart lessons, the play was written. Children in the class were cast in various roles and rehearsals began. The book selections became the focus for the program.

The following excerpt from the script shows the imaginative and creative ideas that developed as a result of the study:

CHILDREN OF OTHER LANDS

NARRATOR: Our class has been studying about children in other lands. We think children are like flowers. If we put all the same flowers in a vase they are very pretty, but if you add different colors, different heights, and different sizes, they all look better.

CHILD: If every child were like every other,
You wouldn't know who was your sister or
brother;
And if every flower looked the same,
"Flower," would have to be each flower's name.

NARRATOR: The first land we are going to visit is *Mexico!*

Various children recited facts learned from their study, illustrated with art work and/or artifacts. They sang a song about the piñata, danced the Mexican hat dance, and the narrator then announced: "Now we are going to show you a film about a Mexican boy named *Pancho* (Weston Woods). The film was shown, dramatically interrupting the children's presentation. France was the next part of the program. Again facts were shared and songs sung. A dramatization of the delightful *Madeline* by Ludwig Bemelmans, with sound effects and musical accompaniment added by the students, was given. The program concluded with a song for the whole assembly to join in singing. This program delighted children in grades two through six—the young children loved it; older ones were amazed at the knowledge gained and the adult tone of the entire production.

A teacher in any school, in any type of situation, can provide frequent experiences for dramatic presentations. Pantomine, mime, and dramatic play need not be as elaborate as the second-grade production cited above; that is only one type of creative dramatics. A cowboy hat, a necktie, a bonnet, or a scarf are simple props that can propel children into the act of acting.

Science, social studies, or mathematics can stimulate instant improvisations:

> How did the cave men walk?
> How do you think Newton looked when he discovered the principle of gravity?
> How does your mother look when she forgot her purse, and she is holding up a long line in the supermarket?

As children approach the upper-elementary grades, formal dramatics can be introduced. Original plays, those children write from other curriculum learnings, or published plays can be produced. In recent years the idea of presenting Shakespeare in the elementary grades has proved very successful. Albert Cullum states that: "The elementary school is the ideal place to introduce Shakespeare." He cites an anecdote of a kindergarten class:

> Once a kindergarten class attended a condensed performance of *The Taming of the Shrew*, which was given by a sixth-grade class, and the arguing and bickering on the stage reminded the little ones of their family life. When I visited them the following year

when they were first-graders and asked them what story they wanted to hear, the response was *The Taming of the Shrew.* Why? They simply wanted to laugh again! School kids come to school to laugh, to be scared, to daydream, to take revenge.[3]

In Fair Lawn, New Jersey, a tremendously successful production of *Macbeth* was presented by fifth-graders.[4] The children read and rewrote the original script keeping, wherever possible, the Elizabethan flavor of the Bards' work. In one scene the script read:

MACBETH: My strong ambition makes me feel that Duncan should be killed. But how can I go ahead with my plan? Lately, Duncan has been speaking well of me.

LADY MACBETH: You fool! Don't you want the high position of King? Are you going to live your life as a coward?

MACBETH: Suppose we fail?

LADY MACBETH: We shall not fail! When King Duncan is asleep, I shall give wine to his guards. They will fall sound asleep, also, and the King will be left unguarded. We shall place the blame on them.

MACBETH: If Duncan is to be assassinated, it would be best to do it quickly. We shall mark the guard's faces with Duncan's blood. This will throw suspicion on them. Everyone will think that they killed the King.

LADY MACBETH: Of course, who will dare think it any

3. Albert Cullum. *Push Back the Desks.* New York: Citation Press, 1967, pp. 82-3.
4. Lee Bennett Hopkins, "No Sighs for Shakespeare," *Catholic School Journal,* February 1968, pp. 52-3.

other way. We, naturally, will show our grief upon his death.

MACBETH: I agree. Aw, but I must hide my face from what my false heart knows.

Knowledge about various cultures can be shared through the use of dramatic presentations. The well-written and beautifully illustrated book, *Pianky, the Great* (Thomas Nelson and Sons, 1965) by E. Harper Johnson, served as a basis for an exciting play created by sixth-grade students in Connecticut. The book tells the stirring story of the great African king who ruled over Kush from 744-712 B.C.

On Pan American Day many programs can be designed to share the rich customs of the South and Latin American countries. In an Indian school in Arizona, children searched out legends from their own and other Indian tribes and presented a moving program that aided in the better understanding and appreciation of Indian cultures and the changes taking place in them.

Government aid has helped to establish many child care centers, Head Start and Follow-Through programs, and after-school community centers in urban areas. Many of these centers have programs that encourage creative dramatic productions. Such experiences enable children to perform a variety of roles and contribute to their future flexibility in real-life situations. Experiences in creative dramatics should be an integral part of every child's training for creative expression heightens sensitivity to both the child's own life problems and his personal relationships with others.

For Further Reading

Beem, Merrill A. "Stepping Stones and Pitfalls in Choral Speaking," *Catholic School Journal,* April 1967, pp. 56-7.

Practical examples of do's and don'ts in planning a choral speaking program are discussed.

Beghe, Theodore L. "And Gladly Teach: Make Room for Literature," *National Elementary Principal,* November 1965, pp. 31-5.

Included is a section entitled "Let Your Pupils Experience the Joys of Choral Reading." An arrangement of Eugene Field's "The Night Wind" also appears.

Camerota, Elaine. "The Play's the Thing to Catch Kid's Minds and Make Them Sing," *Scholastic Teacher,* March 17, 1967, pp. 16-17.

A list of six practical lessons to teach before rehearsals of a formal dramatic play situation begins.

Crimmins, Leonora. "So I Gave Them Shakespeare," *Scholastic Teacher,* March 5, 1965, pp. 12-13.

A California teacher describes a Shakespeare pageant presented by elementary school children.

Cullum, Albert. *Shake Hands with Shakespeare.* New York: Citation Press, 1968.

Adaptations for elementary school children of eight of the Bard's greatest comedies and tragedies. (*Hamlet, Macbeth, Julius Caesar, Romeo and Juliet, The Comedy of Errors, Taming of the Shrew, A Midsummer Night's Dream,* and *The Tempest*). In addition to the plays, there are scene-by-scene vocabulary lists, hints on how to stress the appropriate mood and theme of each play, and simple costuming and staging directions. This paperbound book is available for $3.00; student scripts of the individual plays are 30¢ each or may be purchased in packets of 20 for $5.00.

Diffin, Leslye. "Opening the Door to Poetry," *The Instructor,* October 1966, pp. 33-4.

An example of using dramatic effects in presenting a second-grade poetry program.

Drama with and for Children (OE 33007). Washington, D. C.: U.S. Department of Health, Education and Welfare, 1960.

A good source book of creative dramatic experiences for children in grades kindergarten through high school.

Henry, Mabel Wright. *Creative Experiences in Oral Language.* Champaign, Illinois: National Council of Teachers of English, 1967.

A booklet of reading by experts in the field of language arts, offering many ideas for the classroom teacher of any grade.

Hopkins, Lee Bennett. "No Sighs for Shakespeare," *Catholic School Journal,* February 1968, pp. 52–3.

A description of *Macbeth,* and how it was produced by fifth-graders in a New Jersey elementary school.

Lettvin, Lorelei Joy. "Stories to Dramatize," *Elementary English,* December 1962, pp. 766-9.

A bibliography divided into sections: (1) stories applicable for younger children capable of working in pantomine; (2) tales to be employed for improvisation and narration.

Critical Thinking and the Language Arts
To Think Is To Think

FROM APPALACHIAN ROADWAYS to the streets of Watts, administrators, school teachers, parents, and others concerned with youth constantly utter such comments as:

Tom, you're not *thinking!*
Did you *think* about that Carlos?
Come now, class, *think* this answer through!

Recently the following conversation was overheard while traveling on a New York subway train:

MOTHER: Don't play with the umbrella!
CHILD: Why?
MOTHER: Because you'll hurt someone with it.
CHILD: O.K.! But when we get outside, can I blow the umbrella up?
MOTHER: You're not thinking! You don't *blow* the umbrella up, you *put* it up.
CHILD: Blow it up! 'Cause it goes POP!
MOTHER: No, you say, "Put it up!"
CHILD: Why?
MOTHER: 'Cause that's what they say! Let's go!

"You're not thinking!"

But was this child thinking? He certainly was! He was thinking the same way Tom, Carlos, or the whole class was thinking. Perhaps the thinking process did not produce the correct answer or response wanted by the teacher or the adult, but these children were *thinking*.

In today's society where children are confronted with a knowledge explosion that is almost beyond adults' comprehension, there is a definite need to re-examine thinking and the thinking process and to utilize every opportunity there is to develop clear thinking abilities in children.

Jean Piaget's pioneering works of the 1920's are being critically examined and re-evaluated; the rigid demarcation he drew between the thinking processes of adults and children is no longer completely accepted. Piaget envisoned all children passing through a variety of fixed stages. For him, the egocentric, self-centered child, from the age of one to six or seven, lived in a world of physical sensation and animism, achieving the ability to form concepts and engage in reflective thought only after the age of 11 or 12.

Today it is felt that the individual child must be considered. The stimulation provided by a complex, urban-based society forces many children to emerge from their narrow world at an early age. Even before children enter school life, they actively engage in thinking.

They explore the world about them; in their cribs and play pens they begin to look around and puzzle. They soon select their favorite toy by comparing and analyzing. They begin to think! As children continue to grow and mature, they perceive their world through sensory experiences. They continue to search and to struggle with ideas. They perceive what is going on around them —at home, in school, in the community, and in the world. They begin to be critical of the ideas and the attitudes of others. They start to analyze problems, uncover many different types of solutions, and see relationships in proper perspectives.

This exposure to the trial and error of experience in living, seeing, doing, and trying leads to early concept formation—the ability to synthesize past and present experience and knowledge for use in future situations. The child who comes in contact with parents, teachers, and peers who permit open-minded thought is able to develop as a divergent thinker. Encouragement, opportunity, and experience can provide the key to this process in which a learner discovers that there are many paths to the correct answer.

Teachers in disadvantaged areas have discovered that a nonverbal child can think. Once he is allowed to use his imagination, *to do* rather than solely *memorize*, a child brings his arsenal of experience and intuition to bear and is able to solve problems without the aid of textbook formulae. The essential stimulants have been teachers who encourage, provide opportunities, and believe in the child's ability to succeed. Piaget's work pointed the way to many who now conclude that the ability to learn to think is dependent upon a large number of factors, including mental and chronological age, physical, emotional, and mental state, and the child's experience with his total environment.

To think effectively, however, children must be

taught those skills necessary to develop their thinking abilities. For centuries man has taught man the basic skills for everything. The carpenter's apprentice learned how to measure wood, how to maintain and sharpen his tools, and when and what tool to use at the proper time. The blacksmith learned how to shoe a horse, how to shape the shoe to the hoof, and how long to fire the metal. An apprentice learned the basic skills necessary to his job—in essence he was learning a formula.

In the early periods of education in America, teachers too taught the basic skills—the formula. It was common to find in children's textbooks typical problems such as:

> Three children each have two pieces of string.
> How many pieces of string do the children have
> in all?

A formula was needed to detect the answer to this problem, and this formula was taught and had to be learned —usually without question.

> What do I have to find out?
> What does this problem tell me?
> What do I know from this problem?
> What do I have to do to find out the answer?
> What will the answer be?

This type of thinking—convergent thinking—was taught for decades throughout our schools. It rested upon a narrow, textbook approach to thinking in which children memorized masses of data and learned formulae and then attempted to apply them to relevant situations and problems. The emphasis was on the **what,** rather than the **why?** The carpenter, the blacksmith, and the student learned his lessons in this fashion or he was a failure!

Today we too must teach the basic skills, but we must go further. We must include other factors and we must guide children so that they will understand the **how** and the **why** of problems so they can become divergent thinkers. We must encourage them to find their own formula—to think for themselves. There are many situations that occur in everyone's life in which decisions have to be made, and there is not, and never will be, one formula that will work in each and every one of these situations. For instance:

> Should I accept that new job?
> Should I join the Glee Club or the Camera Club?
> What color should we paint the room?
> What should I make for tonight's dinner?
> Do we really need a color television set?
> What crayon should I use now?
> Should I ask mommy now for the Dr. Dolittle doll, or should I wait until she's in a better mood?
> Should I buy slacks and a jacket, or a suit?
> What can I bring in for "Show and Tell" tomorrow?

Is there a single formula that would apply to this list of life situations? Of course not! Is there only one way to solve the problem about the three children each having two pieces of string? Of course there is!

The formula is out of date! We must teach more than the basic skills of thinking. There are factors other than the basic skills that affect the thinking process and grow out of a child's experiences. These factors—emo-

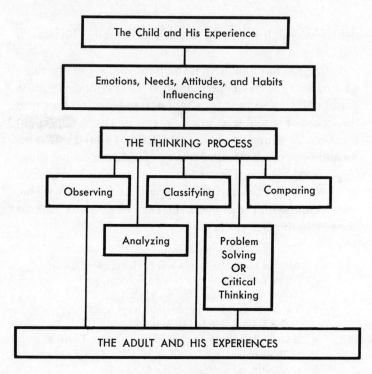

Schema for Thinking

tions, needs, attitudes, and habits—are termed by David
H. Russell, in *Children's Thinking*, as "the motives for
thinking"; they are motives that help to "initiate and
determine the direction of thinking." Suffice to say that
the thinking process cannot be divorced from these motives and that these motives must be brought to the
child's attention. Utilize every opportunity to help the
learner to recognize what skill is needed where—what
he is doing and why—for a child can become cognizant

of the fact that a final decision is only attained when he realizes that such motives can, and will, affect his decisions. Teachers must train youngsters to think for themselves and to think with clarity and precision.

We must encourage free-ranging inquiry and exploration, for these are needed to develop a divergent thinker; this is the type of thinker we must try to produce. Combining thinking skills with language arts experiences is an excellent way of measuring and developing thinking abilities. Through the areas of the language arts thinking abilities can be put into operational terms —listening, speaking, reading, and writing.

The thinking process includes five basic components: observing, classifying, comparing, analyzing, and problem solving or critical thinking.

Observing

Look out the window! What do you see?
I see rain! It looks like the clouds are crying to water the flowers.

• • •

The plants need watering
How can you tell?

You notice, you perceive, you observe!

Countless ways and countless opportunities occur every day to teach children to observe. We can take advantage of such opportunities to develop the sense organs:

> What do you see?
> What do you hear?
> How does that taste?
> How does that feel?
> How does that smell?

Teachers can combine these opportunities with experiments to teach a pattern to follow and to teach how important observation is in relation to the thinking process.

An experiment was tried and tested with a group of second-graders to sharpen their process of observation. The class was motivated to observe the formation of molds by discussing a lemon that was slightly moldy. Question after question was posed, and soon each child had volunteered to bring something from home to observe for the next few days.

> I'll bring in bacon!
> I'll bring cheese!
> I'll bring in some coffee grounds!
> I'll try a carrot!

Thus foodstuffs and materials were brought into class to be experimented with and to be observed. Each child was given a mimeographed form to record his observations if he so chose.

MY (carrot) MOLD		
Date:	What I Saw Today:	Statement about the mold or a picture of the mold.

The children had a continuous experience with their observations. Each child had the opportunity to follow through his own experiment and was able to observe the many other experiments taking place in the classroom. Records were kept, information was gathered by the boys and girls, knowledge sharing took place, and the class learned how to solve a problem using the scientific method. They identified a problem, they collected relevant information in regard to their problem. They organized the information, and they evaluated and compared their experiences with others in the class.

Thinking was going on here; sensory images were being explored. The classroom climate was perfect for learning, and thus powers of observation were increasing, and the children's ability to think critically developed.

What other experiences can be provided for observing? A trip through the school can be an enlightening experience for children. Walk down the halls one morning. When you return to the classroom, discuss the things the children saw, things they had passed by time after time, such as the floors, doors, and the type of material used in the building's construction. Talk about the things they looked at and saw and the things they looked at and did not see. Go back again. This time, however, perceptions will be more acute, more varied. A similar experience can be planned in the neighborhood. The children will be amazed to discover all the things around them that they never observed.

A fourth-grade teacher in a Harlem school planned an interesting walking trip for his class, which combined the observation process with New York City history. The class walked to West 134th Street to the house where Countee Cullen, the famed Negro poet, once lived. They continued to 104 West 135th Street to the Arthur A. Schomberg Collection of the New York Public Library, where more than 36,000 bound volumes, newspapers, and articles are kept, all of which deal with some aspect of Negro history. The children learned that people from all over the country and the world use the resources in this collection. On the next block, at 151-153 136th Street, they saw the site of the Zion church—the mother church of the oldest established Negro church in the United States. The building was designed by the Negro architect, Vertner Tandy. On the way back to the school, the class looked for other interesting buildings by observing cornerstones and markings on apartment houses. The purpose of the excursion was to show the class the uniqueness of the community they live in. Many of the boys and girls had always lived in this immediate neighborhood and yet never observed the rich, historical heritage that surrounded them.

Such a trip can be taken in any neighborhood. It is interesting to see what children can discover from careful observation. Historic sites, homes of interesting community personalities, or places of local importance might be uncovered.

In Arlington, Virginia, one teacher takes her first-grade class to look at the same trees six times during the year. The children spend 15 silent minutes carefully examining the tree. When they return to the classroom, they discuss what they have seen. The teacher records many of their observations, saving them to compare with their next visit. The many learnings that come out of this experience could be utilized on any grade level.

Another teacher asks his fourth-grade class to bring an everyday object to class—a pencil, a milk carton, a saucer, or a brush. These objects become the basis of a lesson on observing the unique qualities of each item. The children are told to look at their object more closely than they ever have before and to rediscover details that they may have taken for granted and never noticed, such as its size, geometric shape, color, texture, and how and why the design fits the purpose the object serves.

"During your next meal notice the color and the shapes of the food you are served," requests a sixth-grade teacher. This becomes the basis for a discussion concerning emotions and attitudes toward food. Questions are generated such as:

> How would you like to eat square peas?
> Do you think you'd like pink mashed potatoes?
> Would green bread be pleasing to you?

This project reveals how we rarely look at or think about common, everyday experiences. In following class discussions the eating habits of other cultures are introduced, and the similarities and differences of food are analyzed. An entire unit on the culture and customs of various groups of people can be evolved from these discussions of Chinese food, Spanish food, and food commonly eaten in various parts of the United States. Where possible, samples of the foods should be brought into the class to encourage many language activities.

Thomas Carlyle, English essayist and philosopher, once remarked:

> Shakespeare says we are creatures that look be-
> fore and after; the more surprising that we do
> not look round a little and see what is passing
> under our very eyes.

Many opportunities and many experiences must be provided so that gradually learners will be looking *and*
seeing. Their percepts will create new awarenesses, and
they will become more conscious of their thinking.
Maybe then they will begin to look round a little and
see what *is* passing under their very eyes!

Classifying

From the time the child enters kindergarten through
the rest of his life, there is need for him to know, understand, and practice the process of classifying.

In the kindergarten and first grades, there are many
opportunities to classify objects—to put things in order
for more efficient use:

> Put all the red crayons in the shoe box.
> Put the puzzles with all the parts on the win-
> dowsill. If there are puzzles with missing
> parts, put them on the top shelf.
> Put the scraps in the paper drawer.
> Place your shell collection on the science table.

Through the grades teachers can offer thousands of
ways to practice this skill.

> Which animal does not belong in this group?
> leopard   cat   tiger   zebra

> Why doesn't the number 32 belong to this set
> of numbers?
> 3   9   15   21   27   32

If a first-grade child sat in our sixth-grade class,
how would a visitor be able to tell that the child
might not belong?

Arrange these circles in various ways.

For example:

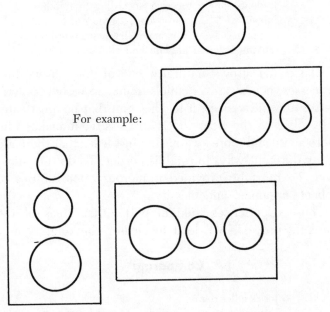

All of the above diagrams have a pattern or
order. Are there other ways to *classify* them?

Why do we call this a classroom?

From the definition of the word *class,* teachers can
provide a spiral-unit approach to thinking throughout the
entire school experience of children.

CLASS (klas, kläs), n. [L. *classis,* class or division
of the Roman people], 1. a number of people
or things grouped together because of certain

likenesses or common traits; kind; sort: as, an inferior class of novels. 2. a group of people considered as a unit according to economics, occupational, or social status . . . 5. a group of students taught together according to standing, subject . . . 11. in biology, a group of animals or plants having a common basic structure and ranking below a *phylum* and above an order.[1]

Classifying grows naturally out of the observation processes; it increases a child's ability to recognize likenesses and differences; it teaches him that he must carefully observe the items he is to classify; it makes him more acute and more aware. He must learn that there are many different ways to establish order. To do this, however, he must be provided numerous opportunities to collect, organize, and classify.

These experiences, tied in with other areas of the thinking process, will lead to clearer thinking.

Comparing

Jose's taller than me!
I've got the same dress on as Marsha!
Your hair is straight, mine is curly!

Children are always comparing—noticing resemblances and differences. Teachers must not let such experiences pass unnoticed but should try to promote, exploit, and utilize them. Simple problems are surefire ways to set young minds in motion.

---

1. David B. Guralink and Joseph H. Friend, eds. *Webster's New World Dictionary of the American Language.* New York: World, 1964, pp. 270.

Compare this goldfish with that one.

Compare the ways we live today to the ways man might be living in the twenty-first century.

How do people travel across the desert in Egypt compared to the way we travel through our city streets?

Compare your answer with Donna's!

How are these two things alike? How are they different?

Working with children in inner-city schools provides rich possibilities for making comparisons. Children coming from the southern and southeast rural areas, from the western plains, or from the many island countries south of the border are often lost and totally confused about their new city environment. Each child, however, no matter what area he comes from, brings with him a rich heritage of culture and history. Many of the natural barriers of communication can be dispelled in school when children are given the opportunity to share and compare information about one another's backgrounds.

In many East Harlem schools, where the majority of the population is Spanish-speaking, and in areas of Hartford, Connecticut, where there are many newly-arrived Spanish children, my colleague Annette Frank Shapiro and I have tried to capitalize on their backgrounds by developing contrasts and comparisons with the children. We encourage teachers to try various activities that will aid in developing the Spanish-American child's concept of self, arouse the mainlander's interest and appreciation for another culture, and implement the teaching of English as a second language.

Comparing, for example, two islands such as Puerto Rico and Manhattan, we suggest the following activities to integrate various critical thinking skills with language arts and social studies enrichment:

START WITH GEOGRAPHIC ORIENTATION

1. On a globe, a world map, and/or a map of the western hemisphere locate islands to survey topographical features; discuss routes of travel to and from New York City; stimulate critical thinking about the relationship of location, climate, and weather, to man's food, clothing, shelter, and work habits.
2. Take a boat or a bus around Manhattan to compare island living. Note the rivers, the bay, the ocean, the shore line, the natural harbor, and the links to other land bodies.
3. Use putty or Plasticene in a large, flat pan, to simulate the geographic features of an island.

TRACE THE HISTORICAL BACKGROUND

1. Compare the discovery and colonization of Puerto Rico and Manhattan.
2. How do the traditions, customs, and languages reflect the influx of the diverse cultures that make up each island?
3. How has the political status of Puerto Rico changed since its earliest colonization? Why?
4. What landmarks reflect the history of Puerto Rico? of New York?

ANALYZE MODERN DAY LIVING

1. What is the population in relation to each island's size? Where are the population centers? Why?
2. What is the economic structure of each island? What goods are exported? imported?
3. Why do both Puerto Rico and New York attract so many tourists? What has tourism done to and for the islands?

DEVELOP ACTIVITIES WITH CHILDREN

1. Take a walk around the neighborhood to see evidences of Spanish culture. Observe language, food products, and plant life as a basis for discussion.
2. Take a trip to botanical gardens to see flora and fauna indigenous to island living. Experiment in the classroom with plant growth by making a terrarium, planting bulbs, citrus fruit seeds, or potatoes. Record the growth on charts or keep daily logs of progress.
3. Plan interviews using questions prepared by the entire class. Children can interview people from Puerto Rico. Parents, local merchants, and professionals may pave the way for further research.
4. Make a large, three-dimensional economic, political, or historical table map showing Puerto Rico in relation to nearby islands.
5. Broadcast the island's news via a classroom television station or over the school broadcasting system.
6. If possible, establish a pen pal or a tape exchange program with a class in Puerto Rico.
7. Make illustrated, individual, or class bilingual dictionaries.

Similar studies and comparisons can be made with any area.

Media provides excellent sources for making comparisons. In one sixth-grade class Gertrude brought in a newspaper with the headline "Anti-American Feelings Mount in European Countries," followed by a sensational, frightening account of the attitudes citizens of Italy, France, and Great Britain felt toward us. After a discussion of the article, it was suggested that children bring in the same story from as many other newspapers as they could. During the next few days, after comparing headlines and news reports, the class discovered the many ways in which the story was slanted, how different writers and different newspapers interpret one incident, and, more important, the need to determine what was fact and what was propaganda.

Reviews in media can also be discussed. Reviews of books, television shows, sports events, and films can be analyzed and compared. Comparing is one of the most direct ways in which thinking takes place, and it is an integral component of the thinking process.

Analyzing

One boy who had listened to several different radio advertisements extolling the "best" cereal was asked by his father which was best. He replied, "There's probably no best cereal; they're just trying to sell more." This boy was seven years old. Such an anecdote is not evidence, but it suggests the possibility that even young children, within the range of their own experiences, may be alertly critical of propaganda.[2]

From the above it can be readily assumed that mass media have great influence on children. Therefore, examining propaganda in advertising offers excellent opportunities for children to develop the ability to analyze and to think critically. Today the mass media are some of the earliest propaganda influences young people encounter; they are constantly confronted with ideas expressed on radio and television. Hours are spent viewing shows that sell "the best cereal," manufacture "the biggest toy," or "make you the strongest when you eat our bread!"

2. David H. Russell. *Children's Thinking*. Boston: Ginn, 1956, pp. 297.

Propaganda appeals to the entire gamut of our emotions. It does so without reference to clear and objective facts. Adults, as well as children, are tempted to jump to conclusions that are the fastest and most feasible ones. We *will* buy "the best cereal" if we hear about it enough; we *will* choose the largest package without stopping to find out how much *really* is inside the container. It is easier to do this than to stop and analyze the many parts of a problem and to arrive at one's own conclusions.

Children must be taught and reminded that pictures and words can have many varied meanings; they must be taught to examine, judge, and be critical of pictures and words. Stop signs should appear when words such as *always, all, never, only, gigantic, fantastic,* or *stupendous* appear in speech or in print.

As early as 1938 the Institute for Propaganda Analysis identified seven basic techniques or types of advertising. They are:

1. Bad names—words with unpleasant connotations.
2. Glad names—words connected with pleasant feelings.
3. Transfer—when you buy a product you'll transfer your feeling to it.
4. Testimonial—well-known person endorses a product.
5. Plain folks—common man.
6. Stacking the cards—telling only a part of the truth.
7. Bandwagon—everybody's doing it.[3]

These seven patterns can be presented to children to initiate a unit on analyzing advertising. Such a unit was tried with a fourth-grade critical thinking group in Fair Lawn, New Jersey.

---

3. Institute for Propaganda Analysis. *Propaganda Analysis*. New York, 1938.

The children were asked to find out what kind of soap was used in their home and why their parents bought specific brands. The recorded session on the following day revealed:

> TONY: My mother buys _____ because it comes in a large bar and they're so many of us using it.
>
> PEARL: We get _____ because my mother says it helps to keep our skin right.
>
> SHARON: Ours is _____ My mother buys it 'cause it's blue and it matches the bathroom.
>
> DONALD: We get _____ 'cause it's cheap!
>
> IRVING: My dad travels a lot and he brings home the little soaps from hotels. We use that!

This session introduced a unit on analyzing advertising in print, on radio, and on television. Children collected advertisements and phrases from radio and television to match the seven basic types of advertising. Charts and booklets were prepared; original television advertisements were written and dramatized for analysis; local stores and supermarkets were visited; and merchants and salesmen were interviewed to see if various merchandise was purchased by consumers because of crash advertising gimmicks such as sales, trading stamp programs, or give-aways.

As a result of an article, "Teaching Children to Analyze Television Advertising,"[4] the Educational Resources Center of Jackson County, Murphysboro, Illinois, decided to teach several experimental units in various

---

4. Lee Bennett Hopkins. "Teaching Children to Analyze Television Advertising," in *Children and TV: Television's Impact on the Child.* Washington, D.C.: Association for Childhood Education International, Bulletin 21-A, 1967, pp. 40-43.

elementary classrooms with the objective of developing a model unit for use throughout the county. A great deal of enthusiasm had been generated among the teachers concerning such a unit, and they followed it up with related units such as selective television viewing and analyzing advertising in other media.

Analyzing is an important skill for all children to learn. Children living in disadvantaged areas particularly should be taught to recognize propaganda influences, for in their immediate communities it is not uncommon to find sign after sign offering sales, discounts, and credit. Prices are greater, interest rates are phenomenally higher, and the sales, discounts, and credits are, in the long run, means to entice the consumer and trap him into thinking that he is getting a bargain.

Ideas too must be analyzed. In *Innovations to Thinking and Doing* (Ginn, 1964), workbooks designed by R. E. Meyers and Paul E. Torrance, many ideas are posed for children to analyze:

> Do you think there ever will be an automobile which can run without oil? (page 70) Why or why not?

> Do you think that a dog with black fur perspires more than one with white fur? Why do you answer as you do? Do you have facts and references to back up your opinions? How could you find out for sure? (page 9)

These kinds of questions and activities are excellent samples of exercises in analyzing, for general knowledge is needed to arrive at a conclusion. Hence, children will have to imagine, explore, research, and discover. Books will have to be found and read, experimentation can be done, and a new interest in the tool that one must use to analyze a problem can be awakened.

An analysis, after a thorough investigation, can be incorrect. It need not necessarily provide a solution to a problem. It is important for children to know and remember this. Analyzing must be thorough. It must dissect each part, uncover every possible solution, weigh the meaning of each word, or detect every line in a drawing.

The child must be made aware that although he may recognize the many pitfalls, like those afforded by the use of propaganda devices, other motives may cause him to give in, or "fall" anyway. A discussion of these motives—the emotions, the needs, the attitudes, the habits—will aid a child in understanding and in evaluating the many ideas he encounters day by day throughout his entire life.

When conclusions are finally reached, they will be the end result of a complete investigation. They will be an analysis, and repeated practice with this process will lead to clearer and more direct thinking.

Problem-Solving or Critical Thinking

One of the most important functions in the thinking process is the ability to solve problems. A problem is defined by David Russell as "a task which a child can understand but for which he does not have an immediate solution. Problem solving, accordingly, is the process by which the child goes from the task or problem as he sees it to a solution which, for him, meets the demands of the problem."[5]

---

5. Russell, *op. cit.*, pp. 251.

Children as well as adults are besieged with problems throughout their lives. They range from the simplest type of decision-making such as: "What shall I buy with my dollar—a game or 100 pieces of bubble gum?" or more significant problems that might affect one's entire way of life.

Problem-solving is a complex process that usually involves many other processes of thinking. In contrast to other areas of the thinking process, problem-solving depends more on precise, careful preparation and confirmation of the result, for usually once the problem is solved, there are few or no alternatives to fall back on.

There is no formula for problem-solving. A person usually varies his own approach to problem-solving from circumstance to circumstance, problem to problem. Two people presented with the same problem might offer different approaches and totally different solutions.

Certain general patterns of the problem-solving process, however, have been determined. These patterns are quite common in educational literature and are usually presented in six basic steps:

1. Identify and understand a problem.
2. Collect all the relevant data and information related to the problem.
3. Select and organize data most relevant to the problem.
4. Formulate a hypothesis.
5. Seek all possible solutions.
6. Select the course that best solves the problem.

Although the above steps are basic, not all these steps would be used to solve every problem nor would they be used in the above order. Each problem must be met with an individual outlook and must be analyzed in a unique way.

Again "the motives for thinking" enter into the solution of a problem, and they may be helpful toward finding the solution or they may curtail the search for the solution. Much practice is needed in the complex process. It is important that the child be given many opportunities to discuss the *whys* and *hows* and *ways* of problem-solving and be taught each of the steps in the problem-solving process. This takes a great deal of time, patience, and understanding, for these skills are not easily acquired. However, these lessons will be valuable ones, and they must be taught and they must be learned, for they are important steps in thinking.

Miss Thea DeBellis, P.S. 96, Bronx, has described the procedures she and her class used in developing the first social studies topics of the year, "The Early Explorers," and the way in which she pinpointed and defined the various aspects of critical thinking:[6]

OUR PROBLEM

We read together, discussed, and set up a time line. We studied the countries involved in the early explorations, the nature of the times, and the qualities, motivations and aims of the people.

We gained a thorough knowledge of the period, of the men, the events, the deeds.

The children wished to go farther. Might they compare the space age today with the age of early explorations?

We discussed the meaning of a problem. We must state our problems as a first step in thinking things through.

WE STATE THE PROBLEM

How can we compare the age of early exploration with the present age of space exploration?

6. Truda T. Weil, ed. *Guiding the Gifted.* New York: Board of Education, Division of Elementary Schools, June 1965, pp. 11-14.

WE GATHER FACTS

Because of the great profusion of materials, the group came to realize that care had to be exercised in the selection of material in order to determine whether it fell within the province of their problem and would contribute to its solution.

WE ORGANIZE INFORMATION

How are we going to put these facts into a form that will give them the greatest possible meaning? The children decided to organize their materials on a chart in the following way:

Problems Facing the Early Explorers and the Space Explorers
Reasons Leading to the Explorations: Then and Now
Motivations of the Men Involved: Then and Now
Motivations of the Countries Involved: Then and Now
The Men and Famous Firsts: Then and Now
Financial Backing: Then and Now
Time: Then and Now
Results: Then and Now
Speed: Then and Now

WE DRAW CONCLUSIONS

The children saw that ships began to be improved because of the many ocean voyages that followed Columbus' historic "first." New knowledge about food came about as well as research into the means of maintaining the health of sailors on long ocean voyages.

The children compared these results with the following present-day explorations: advances in mapping the moon, improved space vehicles, new navigational instruments, and research in connection with space foods and medicine.

This study led the children to conclude that there was a similarity between the results of early explorations and those of today's space explorations and that present research and experimentation will very likely lead to improving living conditions for human beings in the world of tomorrow.

Each child realized that he had gathered much more information than he could possibly use and that because of the limitations of the chart, each piece of information had to be carefully selected and greatly abbreviated. This planned emphasis upon some of the important steps leading to critical thinking helped build a foundation for the solution of more complex problems.

While these skills are being mastered, the child will see himself becoming more flexible in seeking solutions to the many problems he encounters. It is necessary to encourage children to try solving problems—not only the problem in the mathematics textbook but real, living problems, the life experiences that all children have within easy grasp.

Miss Levine, the teacher at the chalkboard, was explaining a mathematics problem and was overjoyed to see her slowest student giving undivided attention.
"You're so interested, Charles, I'm sure you want to ask some questions?"
"Naw, only one," drawled Charles. "Where do the figgers go when you rub 'em off that board?"

Charles posed a new problem—probably one much more interesting than the one Miss Levine had presented. This could be the impetus for a whole new unit —perhaps a unit on problem-solving!

Afterthoughts

Observing, classifying, comparing, analyzing, and problem-solving are all interrelated parts of the thinking process. For centuries philosophers have speculated about the workings of the human mind, and the whats, whys, and hows of thought processes are still being pondered by thinkers and scientists today.

One of the most important and influential men in America to study the subject of thinking was John Dewey. His text, entitled *How We Think* (Heath, 1910), encouraged many more theorists in the field to explore the thinking process (see chronological list at the end of this chapter). Many varied and different hypotheses have been expounded since 1910; some are excellent, some are fair, and some will forever languish by the wayside.

One big question recurs time and time again throughout the literature—can we teach children how to think? The answer is emphatically no! No one can teach another human being how to think. Our aim, as educators, should be **to help children to learn to think**—to learn the thinking process—not to teach them how to think. Such learning cannot be developed in connection with just one subject. It cannot, for example, be related only to scientific experiments or mathematical problems. It must be correlated with the entire curriculum—with subject matter areas as well as personal relationships such as getting along with others, sharing, and behaving in the classroom. It must be developed continually and repetitively in the entire school curriculum.

We must focus our attention on aiding individual children to make use of the natural abilities they have within them. We must teach the skills and mechanics of the thinking process. We must cultivate that which a child uses naturally and will continue to use in his everyday life. Then the learning situation will be more realistic—and so will our goals. Then we can expect results that are within reach. And when the child matures into an adolescent and the adolescent matures into an adult, we will have succeeded in producing a thinking adult.

We have a long way to go, but we can get there!

Perhaps one day when a child says: "Blow up the umbrella" or "Where do the figgers go when you rub 'em off?" adults will not wince or scowl or quickly respond with: "You're not thinking!"

Perhaps they will understand that these statements are just as valid, or even more so, as when a child responds: "Two plus two is four" or "1492. It was 1492 when Columbus discovered America."

Perhaps they will learn to accept the multitude of divergent ways of thinking that our fast-changing world will continue to require.

Perhaps they will begin to think much more about thinking.

Perhaps teachers should too!

Perhaps!

For Further Reading

Allen, Adrianna. "Five Year Olds Can Think," *Elementary English,* January 1963, pp. 72–4+.

An informative article utilizing the everyday experiences of kindergarten children to spark discussion periods and to get them thinking critically and creatively. The article is filled with fine suggestions.

Bingham, Alma. *Improving Children's Facility in Problem Solving.* New York: Bureau of Publications, Teachers College, Columbia University, 1958.

Many practical suggestions are offered. Anecdotes are cited followed by ways to deal with common situations in classrooms.

Hopkins, Lee Bennett. "Teaching Children to Analyze Television Advertising," in *Children and TV: Television's Impact on the Child*. Washington, D.C.: Association for Childhood Education International, Bulletin 21-A, 1967, pp. 40–43.

Suggestions are offered for teaching a unit on television advertising to various grade levels. Introducing the unit, pupil activities, culminating activities, and teacher-resources are included. Available in paperback for $1.25.

Simon, Sidney B., and Lieberman, Phyllis. "Analyzing Advertising: An Approach to Critical Thinking," *National Elementary Principal*, September 1966, pp. 16–18.

Five advertisements of well-known products are discussed. Ideas contained in this article can be adapted to various grade levels.

Usery, Mary Lou. "Critical Thinking Through Children's Literature," *Elementary English*, February 1966, pp. 115–8+.

A model of critical thinking and means of evaluating the teaching of critical thinking as related to children's literature in the primary grades.

Wolfe, Evelyn. "Advertising and the Elementary Language Arts." *Elementary English*, January 1965, pp. 42–4+.

A program developed in Pleasant Hill, California, with sixth-grade students in an accelerated language arts program is discussed. Many creative ideas offered.

A Chronological List of Texts on Thinking

1910 John Dewey. *How We Think*. Boston: Heath.
1912 Irving Elgar Miller. *The Psychology of Thinking*. New York: Macmillan.
1924 Julius Borass. *Teaching to Think*. New York: Macmillan.
1926 Jean Piaget. *The Language and Thought of the Child*. New York: Harcourt.

1933 John Dewey. *How We Think: A Restatement of the Relation of Reflective Thinking to the Educative Process.* Boston: Heath.

1936 Percival M. Symonds. *Education and the Psychology of Thinking.* New York: McGraw-Hill.

1942 Howard R. Anderson, ed. *Teaching Critical Thinking in the Social Studies.* Washington, D.C.: National Education Association.

1946 Max Black. *Critical Thinking: An Introduction to Logic and Scientific Thinking.* Englewood Cliffs, New Jersey: Prentice-Hall.

1955 David H. Russell. *Children's Thinking.* Boston: Ginn.

1961 Jerome S. Bruner. *The Process of Education.* Cambridge: Harvard University Press.

1965 John Holt. *How Children Fail.* New York: Pitman.

1967 Louis Rath and others. *Teaching for Thinking: Theory and Application.* Columbus, Ohio: Charles E. Merrill.

The Urban and Disadvantaged Child:
A Booklist for Children

Appendix I

Kindergarten, First and Second Grades

Blos, Joan W. *"It's Spring," She Said.* New York: Knopf, 1968.
   Tells of spring coming to the city and the affect it has on various people. The illustrations by Julie Maas vividly capture the city's people and places.

Bourne, Miriam Anne. *Raccoons Are for Loving.* New York: Random House, 1968.
   Josephine, a young Negro girl who lives in the city, loves to hear Grannie tell of her childhood in South Carolina—especially about the raccoon that came out of the woods. When the class takes a field trip to the country, Josephine sees a real raccoon. A good text with illustrations by Marian Morton.

Cherr, Pat, and Keats, Ezra Jack. *My Dog Is Lost.* New York: Crowell, 1960.
   Juanito, a young Puerto Rican child, has lost his dog somewhere in the huge confines of bustling New York City. His travels to Chinatown, Park Avenue, and Harlem and the people he meets make for a warm and humorously written story.

Clifford, Eth and David. *Your Face Is a Picture*. Indianapolis: Seale, 1967.

Photographs of children portray the various moods they have.

Ets, Marie Hall. *Gilberto and the Wind*. New York: Viking, 1963.

A story of Gilberto and his trials and tribulations with Mr. Wind. Mr. Wind can be kind, or destructive, and sometimes just a companion to a young child.

Freeman, Don. *Corduroy*. New York: Viking, 1968.

Corduroy is a bear who once lived in a toy department of a big store. One day Lisa, a young Negro girl, buys him for her own. This picture book stresses a universal theme—the love of a child for a doll.

Gaeddart, Lou Ann. *Noisy Nancy Norris*. New York: Doubleday, 1965.

Noisy Nancy Norris has to become a little quieter or else her family will be evicted from their apartment house. This delightful story will appeal to young children who know how hard it is to be quiet. Illustrations are humorously done by Gioia Fiammenghi and show Nancy's many moods and mischievous doings.

Hawkinson, John and Lucy. *Little Boy Who Lives Up High*. Chicago: Whitman, 1967.

A picture book about Ricky, a young Negro child whose home is in a high-rise apartment building. An imaginative yet simple story to help children understand the many ways we live.

Horvath, Betty. *Hooray for Jasper*. New York: Watts, 1966.
———. *Jasper Makes Music*. New York: Watts, 1967.

Jasper is a young Negro boy in a middle-class family. Illustrations in brown and white by Ferman Rocker are large and detailed.

Keats, Ezra Jack. *The Snowy Day*.* New York: Viking, 1962.
———. *Whistle for Willie** New York: Viking, 1962.
———. *Peter's Chair*. New York: Harper, 1967.

* Available in paperback from Scholastic Book Services, Inc., 904 Sylvan Avenue, Englewood Cliffs, New Jersey 07632.

————. *A Letter to Amy.* Harper, 1968.

In each of these stories Peter, a young Negro child, experiences simple adventures which any child might engage in. In *The Snowy Day*, winner of the 1963 Caldecott Medal, Peter romps in the newly fallen snow; in *Whistle for Willie* he learns how to whistle for his pet dog; *Peter's Chair* deals with sibling rivalry—Peter has a new baby sister and resents it; in *A Letter to Amy*, Peter invites Amy, the only girl, to his birthday party.

Kempner, Carol. *Nicholas.* New York: Simon and Schuster, 1968.

Nicholas, a young Negro child, gets lost on the subway train. He ends up in a zoo where he meets a balloon man who returns him safely home.

Levenson, Dorothy. *The Magic Carousel.* New York: Parents', 1967.

At Christmas time Dana and Lisa go to Central Park in New York City with their daddy. When they take a ride on the carousel, the horses gallop off and take them on a fantasy journey through the city. Illustrations by Ati Forberg are exciting and highly artistic.

Lexau, Joan M. *I Should Have Stayed in Bed.* New York: Harper, 1965.

Sam, a young Negro child, begins a day of constant trials and tribulations, feeling that if he had stayed in bed he would not have found himself in so many predicaments. This is an easy-to-read book illustrated by Syd Hoff.

Manneheim, Grete. *The Two Friends.* New York: Knopf, 1968.

The two friends are Jenny, a young Negro girl, and Nancy, a white girl, who meet in Mrs. Oliver's kindergarten. The book is illustrated in excellent photographs taken by the author.

Pitt, Valerie. *Let's Find Out About the City.* New York: Watts, 1968.

An easy-to-read introduction to city life. Illustrations by Sheila Granda excitingly depict the city's many moods and tempos.

Ressner, Philip. *At Night*. New York: Dutton, 1967.

"At night, when most children are asleep, many things are different . . . Darkness is all around, like the air." This text explores the feeling of nighttime in a city neighborhood through simple text and interesting photographs by Charles Pratt.

Scott, Ann Herbert. *Big Cowboy Western*. New York: Lothrop, 1966.

Martin receives a cowboy suit for his fifth birthday and sets out to be a "big cowboy" in the big city. Martin is a Negro child who lives in an urban housing development. Illustrations by Richard W. Lewis are in black and white and color and vividly capture the spirit of this delightful picture book.

————. *Let's Catch a Monster*. New York: Lothrop, 1967.

Martin is featured again. This time he sets out with his friends to catch a monster on Halloween. The two-color illustrations are by H. Tom Hall.

Simon, Norma. *What Do I Say?* Chicago: Whitman, 1967.

A very simple book about a Puerto Rican child living in a large American city. The format is simply "I talk on the telephone. What do I say?—Hello!" This text is also available in an English-Spanish edition. Both volumes contain a note about the philosophy of the text.

Sonneborn, Ruth. *The Lollipop Party*. New York: Viking, 1967.

Tomas, a very young Puerto Rican child, faces the plight of being left alone in his apartment for the first time. This charming story is aided greatly by warm and sensitive illustrations by Brinton Turkle.

————. *7 In a Bed*. New York: Viking, 1968.

Juanita, Maria, Carlos, Pedro, Tomas, Ana, and Manuelo—all new arrivals to America—temporarily have to share one bed. The text is warmly illustrated by Don Freeman.

Tresselt, Alvin. *Wake Up, City!* New York: Lothrop, 1957.

The hustle and bustle of the city as it wakes up in the morning is depicted. Illustrations are by the Caldecott Award winner Roger Duvoisin.

Wilson, Julia. *Becky.* New York: Crowell, 1966.

Becky wants to buy a doll that costs $2.00 more than she has received for her birthday. This is a tender, fanciful tale of a working-class Negro mother-daughter relationship.

Yashima, Taro. *Crow Boy.* New York: Viking, 1955.

Chibi, a Japanese boy, faces the problem of being accepted in a new environment.

————. *Umbrella.* New York: Viking, 1958.

An appealing story of a three-year-old Japanese girl born in New York, who longs for a rainy day to come so that she may use her new umbrella and boots.

Zemach, Harve, adapter. *Mommy, Buy Me a China Doll.* New York: Follett, 1966.

An adaptation of an Ozark's child song done in beautifully designed red, brown, and yellow illustrations.

Third and Fourth Grades

Bacemeister, Rhoda W. *The People Downstairs and Other City Stories.* New York: Coward-McCann, 1964.

"A Word from the Author" states: "This is a book about little children, native and foreign born, white, Negro, Oriental, Jewish, Catholic, and Protestant, healthy and physically handicapped, living together in a crowded section of a big city." In "Fire Escape Weather," little Ronnie Butler plays under an open hydrant on a hot summer's day; Juan, newly arrived from Puerto Rico, witnesses his first snowfall; Cho Leung buys his mother a light, green teapot with the picture of the bamboo on it in "Happy Year of the Dog."

Burchardt, Nellie. *Project Cat*. New York: Watts, 1966.

Betsy, a Negro child, and her friends find and secretly care for a cat, for pets were not allowed in the city housing project. Illustrations by Fermin Rocker add greatly to this urban story.

Carlson, Bernice Wells. *You Know What? I Like Animals*. New York: Abingdon Press, 1967.

Since NO ANIMALS ALLOWED is posted in the lobby of Joey's apartment house, he invents pretend pets.

Estes, Eleanor. *The 100 Dresses*. New York: Harcourt, 1944.

Wanda Petronski wears the same dress to school every day, yet she has "100 dresses at home!" The tauntings by her schoolmates lead to many learnings of understanding and tolerance.

Ets, Marie Hall. *Bad Boy, Good Boy*. New York: Crowell 1967.

Roberto, a Mexican boy, is one of five children in a poor family living in California. When family problems arise, Roberto becomes further confused and quite hard to cope with. This is a realistic account of a young child's problems in adjusting to life.

Grifalconi, Ann. *City Rhythms*. New York: Bobbs-Merrill, 1965.

A young boy learns the sounds of the big city and makes them part of his play. Large, colorful illustrations by the author offer many possibilities for discussion about city life.

Hayes, Florence. *Skid*. New York: Houghton, 1948.

Skid moved from the South to Connecticut and finds he is the only Negro boy in his new school.

Hill, Elizabeth Starr. *Evan's Corner*. New York: Holt, 1967.

Evan, a small Negro boy living in New York's Harlem, longed for a place of his own. He explains: "I want a chance to be lonely . . . In my own way. In my own corner." Soft water-color illustrations by Nancy Grossman vividly portray the city and its many faces.

Lewiton, Mina. *Candita's Choice*. New York: Harper, 1959.

How does a Puerto Rican child feel coming to live in an inner-city? How does the school differ? How is the child received by her peer group? This book realistically portrays the problems of the immigrant in a new environment.

Lexau, Joan M. *Benjie*. New York: Dial, 1964.

Benjie is a shy little lad who sets out in the city on an adventure to find one of his grandmother's lost earrings. The story is one young children will love to read or listen to.

Molarsky, Osmund. *The Song of the Empty Bottles*. New York: Walck, 1968.

This is the story of Thaddeus and how he earns enough money to buy a used guitar. The book is illustrated by Tom Feelings.

Selden, George. *The Cricket in Times Square*. New York: Farrar, Straus, 1960.

A beautiful modern-day tale of Tucker Mouse and Harry the Cat and how they initiate Chester, a country cricket, into the way-of-life in New York City. Illustrations by Garth Williams are perfect. The text was a runner-up for the 1961 Newbery Award.

Speevak, Yetta. *Spider Plant*. New York: Atheneum, 1965.

The story of Carmen, a member of a newly arrived Puerto Rican family and the adjustments she must make to a small, dark apartment in New York City. A spider plant helps to make her life a little brighter.

York, Carol Beach. *The Blue Umbrella*. New York: Watts, 1968.

Joanna has a great deal to do during the summer months in the busy city, but much of it is done indoors. A good portrayal of urban life through characters young readers will enjoy.

Fifth and Sixth Grades and Mature Readers

Bonham, Frank. *Durango Street.** New York: Dutton, 1965.

The story of teenage gangs and their inter-gang warfare on city streets.

---

* Available in paperback from Scholastic Book Services, Inc., 904 Sylvan Avenue, Englewood Cliffs, New Jersey 07632.

Burch, Robert. *Queenie Peavy*. New York: Viking, 1966.

Queenie Peavy is a young girl who grows up in Depression-ridden rural Georgia. A skillfully told story; winner of the Child Study Association Book Award for 1966.

Carunungan, Calso Al. *Like a Brave Man*. New York: Farrar, 1960.

This text tells of Crispin, a Filipino boy who comes to New York City to find conditions surprising and, at times, frightening.

Cohen, Robert. *The Color of Man*. New York: Random House, 1968.

A text that answers such questions as: "What Is Color?" and "Where Does Color Come From?" Excellent black and white photographs by Ken Hyman are used to illustrate the difficult concepts.

Coleman, Hila. *The Girl from Puerto Rico*. New York: Morrow, 1961.

Felicidad, a 16-year-old girl, moves to New York City with her mother and her two brothers. The problems she faces there make her long for her homeland.

Coles, Robert. *Dead End School*. Boston: Little, Brown, 1968.

Dr. Coles tells the story of Jim, his family, and friends and their problems of integration in an American city. Norman Rockwell's few illustrations add to the realism of the text.

Gates, Doris. *North Fork*. New York: Viking, 1945.

Drew Saunders, a 13-year-old orphan, finds what it is like to be one of a minority when he goes to an Indian village.

Gregor, Arthur S. *How the World's First Cities Began*. New York: Dutton, 1967.

This text gives the reader insight that will enable him to understand his own city environment. An interesting text tracing the long and gradual development of the first cities.

Jackson, Jesse. *Tessie*. New York: Harper, 1968.

Tessie lives in Harlem and her problems begin when she wins

a scholarship to Hobbe, an exclusive private school in east Manhattan. Line drawings by Harold James are included.

Konigsburg, E. L. *From the Mixed-Up Files of Mrs. Basil E. Frankweiler.* New York: Antheneum, 1967.

This is the 1968 winner of the Newbery Award. It tells of two suburban children who run away from home to live in New York's Metropolitan Museum of Art. The text can be used to spark many discussions or just read aloud to delight readers in the upper-elementary grades. Illustrations by the author are excellent.

Lawson, John. *You Better Come Home with Me.* New York: Crowell, 1966.

A fantasy about an Appalachian boy who wanders from the mountains to settle in a town populated with a scarecrow, a fox, a witch, and a snowman—as well as people.

Lettau, Edward, and Wakin, Edward. *At the Edge of Harlem.* New York: Morrow, 1965.

Illustrated in photographs, the book tells of a middle-class Negro family and how they live. A good portrayal of modern Negro life.

Lexau, Joan. *Striped Ice Cream.* Philadelphia: Lippincott, 1968.

A story of a real family's ups and downs, the quarrels and making-ups, and of Becky, a young Negro child, and her happy birthday. The book is illustrated by John Wilson in black and white drawings.

Neville, Emily. *It's Like This Cat.** New York: Harper, 1963.

This Newbery Award winner of 1964 tells of Dave Mitchell's stray tomcat named Cat. Set in contemporary New York, this book should delight older readers in the upper grades. A warm story about our current generation.

Schwartz, Alvin. *The City and Its People: The Story of One City's Government.* New York: Dutton, 1967.

Using Trenton, New Jersey, as a model, the author describes

---

* Available in paperback from Scholastic Book Services, Inc., 904 Sylvan Avenue, Englewood Cliffs, New Jersey 07632.

the workings of a city. A factual text filled with excellent photographs and diagrams.

Seredy, Kate. *A Tree for Peter*. New York: Viking, 1941.

A mysterious stranger comes to shanty town, bringing faith and happiness to a lame boy. Excellent illustrations.

Shotwell, Louisa. *Adam Bookout*. New York: Viking, 1967.

After Adam's parents are killed in a plane crash, he leaves Oklahoma to live with his relatives in Brooklyn, New York. A well told story of boys and girls living together in a mixed, urban neighborhood.

————. *Roosevelt Grady.* ** New York: World, 1963.

An excellent story about Roosevelt, the young son of a migrant worker's family. Illustrations in black and white by Peter Burchard add to this sympathetic, realistic account.

Stolz, Mary. *A Wonderful, Terrible Time*. New York: Harper, 1967.

Mady Guthrie and Sue Ellen Forrest, two Negro children, are inseparable friends who live across the hall from each other in a racially mixed neighborhood. A visit from a stranger results in a surprise that is both wonderful and terrible. This text is a 1967 American Library Association Notable Book.

Weik, Mary Hays. *Jazz Man*. New York: Atheneum, 1966.

Runner-up for the 1967 Newbery Award, this story tells of Zeke, a boy who is uprooted from the South to live in a Harlem tenement. Poor parent relationships and their effect on a child's life are vividly depicted. Fine woodcuts by Ann Grifalconi, the author's daughter.

** Available in paperback from Tempo Books, Grosset and Dunlap, Inc., 51 Madison Avenue, New York, New York 10010.

Award Winning Children's Books

Appendix II

Caldecott Award Winning Books

The Caldecott Medal is named in honor of Randolph Caldecott (1846–1886), an English illustrator of children's books. The Medal is presented annually by a committee of the Children's Service Division of the American Library Association to "the artist of the most distinguished American picture book for children." The list below cites the year the book received the award, the title, the illustrator, the author when different from the illustrator, and the publisher.

1938 *Animals of the Bible: A Picture Book.* Dorothy O. Lathrop. Text selected from the King James Bible by Helen Dean Fish. Lippincott.

1939 *Mei Lei.* Thomas Handforth. Doubleday.

1940 *Abraham Lincoln.* Ingri and Edgar Parin d'Aulaire. Doubleday.

1941 *They Were Strong and Good.* Robert Lawson. Viking.

1942 *Make Way for Ducklings.* Robert McCloskey. Viking.

1943 *The Little House.* Virginia Lee Burton. Houghton.

1944 *Many Moons*. Louis Slobodkin. Text by James Thurber. Harcourt.

1945 *Prayer for a Child*. Elizabeth Orton Jones. Text by Rachel Field. Macmillan.

1946 *The Rooster Crows*. Maud and Miska Petersham. Macmillan.

1947 *The Little Island*. Leonard Weisgard. Text by Golden MacDonald. Doubleday.

1948 *White Snow, Bright Snow*. Roger Duvoisin. Text by Alvin Tresselt. Lothrop.

1949 *The Big Snow*. Berta and Elmer Hader. Macmillan.

1950 *Song of the Swallows*. Leo Politi. Scribner.

1951 *The Egg Tree*. Katherine Milhous. Scribner.

1952 *Finders Keepers*. Nicolas (Mordvinoff). Text by Will (William Lipkind.) Harcourt.

1953 *The Biggest Bear*. Lynd Ward. Houghton.

1954 *Madeline's Rescue*. Ludwig Bemelmans. Viking.

1955 *Cinderella*. Marcia Brown. Text by Charles Perrault. Harper.

1956 *Frog Went A-Courtin'*. Feodor Rojankovsky. Text by John Langstaff. Harcourt.

1957 *A Tree Is Nice*. Marc. Simont. Text by Janice May Udry. Harper.

1958 *Time of Wonder*. Robert McCloskey. Viking.

1959 *Chanticleer and the Fox*. Barbara Cooney. Crowell.

1960 *Nine Days to Christmas*. Marie Hall Ets. Text by Marie Hall Ets and Aurora Labastilda. Viking.

1961 *Baboushka and the Three Kings*. Nicolas Sidjakov. Text by Ruth Robbins. Parnassus.

1962 *Once a Mouse*. Marcia Brown. Scribner.

1963 *The Snowy Day*. Ezra Jack Keats. Viking.

1964 *Where the Wild Things Are*. Maurice Sendak. Harper.

1965 *May I Bring a Friend. Beni Montresor*. Text by Beatrice Schenk de Regniers. Atheneum.

1966 *Always Room for One More*. Nonny Hogrogian. Text by Sorche Nic Leodhas. Holt.

1967 *Sam, Bangs and Moonshine*. Evaline Ness. Holt.

1968 *Drummer Hoff*. Ed Emberley. Text by Barbara Emberley. Prentice-Hall.

Newbery Award Winning Books

The Newbery Medal is named in honor of John Newbery, an eighteenth century bookseller and publisher. The Medal is presented annually by a committee of the Children's Service Division of the American Library Association to "the author of the most distinguished contribution to American literature for children." The list below cites the year the book received the award, the title, the author, and publisher.

1922 *The Story of Mankind*. Hendrik Van Loon. Boni & Liveright.
1923 *The Voyages of Doctor Dolittle*. Hugh Lofting. Lippincott.
1924 *The Dark Frigate*. Charles Boardman Hawes. Little, Brown.
1925 *Tales from Silver Lands*. Charles J. Finger. Doubleday.
1926 *Shen of the Sea*. Arthur Bowie Chrisman. Dutton.
1927 *Smoky, the Cowhorse*. Will James. Scribner.
1928 *Gay Neck*. Dhan Gopal Mukerji. Dutton.
1929 *Trumpeter of Krakow*. Eric P. Kelly. Macmillan.
1930 *Hitty, Her First Hundred Years*. Rachel Field. Macmillan.
1931 *The Cat Who Went to Heaven*. Elizabeth Coatsworth, Macmillan.
1932 *Waterless Mountain*. Laura Adams Armer. McKay.
1933 *Young Fu of the Upper Yangtze*. Elizabeth Foreman. Holt.
1934 *Invincible Louisa*. Cornelia Meigs. Little, Brown.
1935 *Dobry*. Monica Shannon. Viking.
1936 *Caddie Woodlawn*. Carol Ryrie Brink. Macmillan.
1937 *Roller Skates*. Ruth Sawyer. Viking.
1938 *The White Stag*. Kate Seredy. Viking.
1939 *Thimble Summer*. Elizabeth Enright. Holt.
1940 *Daniel Boone*. James H. Daugherty. Viking.
1941 *Call It Courage*. Armstrong Sperry. Macmillan.
1942 *The Matchlock Gun*. Walter D. Edmonds. Dodd, Mead.
1943 *Adam of the Road*. Elizabeth Janet Gray. Viking.

1944 *Johnny Tremain.* Esther Forbes. Houghton.
1945 *Rabbit Hill.* Robert Lawson. Viking.
1946 *Strawberry Girl.* Lois Lenski. Lippincott.
1947 *Miss Hickory.* Carolyn Sherwin Bailey. Viking.
1948 *The Twenty-One Balloons.* William Pene du Bois. Viking.
1949 *King of the Wind.* Marguerite Henry. Rand McNally.
1950 *The Door in the Wall.* Marguerite de Angeli. Doubleday.
1951 *Amos Fortune, Free Man.* Elizabeth Yates. Dutton.
1952 *Ginger Pye.* Eleanor Estes. Viking.
1953 *Secret of the Andes.* Ann Nolan Clark. Viking.
1954 *. . . And Now Miguel.* Joseph Krumgold. Crowell.
1955 *The Wheel on the School.* Meindert De Jong. Harper.
1956 *Carry On, Mr. Bowditch.* Jean Lee Latham. Houghton.
1957 *Miracles on Maple Hill.* Virginia Sorensen. Harcourt.
1958 *Rifles for Waitie.* Harold Keith. Crowell.
1959 *The Witch of Blackbird Pond.* Elizabeth George Speare. Houghton.
1960 *Onion John.* Joseph Krumgold. Crowell.
1961 *Island of the Blue Dolphins.* Scott O'Dell. Houghton.
1962 *The Bronze Bow.* Elizabeth George Speare. Houghton.
1963 *A Wrinkle in Time.* Madeline L'Engle. Farrar.
1964 *It's Like This, Cat.* Emily Neville. Harper.
1965 *Shadow of a Bull.* Maia Wojciechowska. Atheneum.
1966 *I, Juan de Pareja.* Elizabeth Borten de Treviño. Farrar.
1967 *Up a Road Slowly.* Irene Hunt. Follett.
1968 *From the Mixed-up Files of Mrs. Basil E. Frankweiler.* E. L. Konigsburg. Atheneum.

Outstanding Volumes of Negro Poetry
Appendix III

Adoff, Arnold, ed. *I Am the Darker Brother*. New York: Macmillan, 1968. (Hardcover and paperback editions.)
This is an anthology of modern poems that is timely and well organized.

Bontemps, Arna, comp. *Golden Slippers*. New York: Harper, 1941.
One of the first anthologies of Negro poetry for boys and girls.

Brooks, Gwendolyn. *Bronzeville Boys and Girls*. New York: Harper, 1956.
This is an original collection of poetry by the first Negro poet ever to win the Pulitzer Prize. The book for young readers offers a new and engaging look into the lives of children living in the crowded conditions of an American inner city.

Doob, Leo W., ed. *A Crocodile Has Me by the Leg*. New York: Walker, 1967.
The rhythms of African folklore are presented in this handsome volume. Solomon Wangboje's bold black and red woodcuts add to the tone of this volume.

Dunbar. Paul Lawrence. *Complete Poems*. New York: Dodd, Mead, 1913.

This popular collection contains the complete works of this famous poet.

Hayden, Robert, ed. *Kaleidoscope: Poems by American Negro Poets*. New York: Harcourt, 1967.

A collection of poems for older readers, "chosen for literary value rather than for their significance as an expression of social protest or racial struggle."

Hughes, Langston. *The Dream Keeper and Other Poems*. New York: Knopf, 1932.

A selection of 60 poems by one of the best-loved Negro poets.

―――. *The Panther and the Lash*. New York: Knopf, 1967.

Seventy poems reflecting the racial turmoil of the 1960's. A volume for mature readers.

Rollins, Charlemae Hill. *Christmas Gif'*. Chicago: Follett, 1963.

Christmas poems, songs, and stories written by and about Negroes and collected by Miss Rollins.